In Black & White

The True Story of
an Interracial Couple in America

By Zosia Gorbaty with Chaka Zulu

Printed in the United States of America
Published by Zosia Gorbaty, Z & Z Publishing
https://zujitsu.net
First Edition
ISBN: 979-8-9996809-0-7

Front Cover Photo by: Greg Thorne
Back Cover Photo by: Tino Gordon
Cover Art Graphic Design by: Jessie Buchanan
Edited by: Jamie Kristen

Dedication

This book is dedicated to every interracial couple who has prevailed through adversity to prove that LOVE WINS!

Foreword

By Alan Onickel

The answer to that age old question, what happens when you mix a Harlem born Black man raised by his St. Thomas born mother after his father was hospitalized due to PTSD suffered while serving in the U.S. Army during WWII, with a Vienna born White woman raised in Manhattan by Polish Holocaust survivors whose father also suffered from PTSD, can now be found!

In Black & White, by Zosia Gorbaty, the above mentioned woman, gives us the answer, with amazing accounts of the awesome adventures that she and Chaka Zulu, the above mentioned man, have experienced and endured, over the past 44 years.

The 1st section, as told by Zulu in interviews with Gorbaty, begins in 1938 and tells the unfortunately too common story of the limits forced on him by the overt racism of that time. It then, amongst other roads taken, follows him through his journey in the US Marines and the many martial arts systems that led to the creation of his martial arts system of Zujitsu Ryu.

In the 2nd section Gorbaty recounts how her parents survived the horrors of the Holocaust while losing most of their families before emigrating to the US with her. Amongst the many memories she shares are tales of her time at the prestigious HS of Music & Art, her " hippie" years in San Francisco, her introduction to yoga, obtaining her Master's degree from New York University, traveling solo through Europe, and her introduction to Karate which eventually led her to Chaka Zulu.

The 3rd section gives us insight as to how Zujitsu came about, and some of its unique exercises and perspectives. It also tells of how Zulu and Gorbaty got together, overcame obstacles, eventually married, and their journey sharing Zujitsu with students around the world. This included schools and organizations throughout the U.S. as well as St. Thomas, Israel, and even China. Any doubts about the efficacy of this hybrid self-defense based martial art were put to rest during countless demonstrations and workshops. Their visit to the world renowned Shaolin Temple was a highlight.

I have to admit my partiality to Zujitsu. Though I'm a 1st degree black belt in Tang Soo Do and I studied Oyama karate for 4 years, I've been a student of Zujitsu for over 25 years. To those thinking martial arts are just about learning how to hurt others, I want to share my story. Just before I was to test for my 1st degree black belt I was almost killed in a car accident while working in S. Africa. After waking up from a short coma I had to live back with my parents in Detroit for almost a year while relearning how to walk, talk, and generally take care of myself. After being there for a few months, one day I got a package in the mail. It contained my black belt and certificate. Receiving that package motivated me to work that much harder in the many different painful physical and mental daily therapies necessary in order to regain the functions that eventually allowed me to return to my life in NYC where I would be tested.

Alan Onickel is an Internationally renowned performer, teacher and choreographer. Author of *Babblings From A Battered Brain*, 5th Degree Black Belt Zujitsu Ryu

Foreword

By Dr. Michelle Manu

There are some lives that stand as quiet testaments to courage, mastery, and devotion. My dear friend Zosia is one such life. She is a martial artist of rare discipline and strength, a musician whose hands speak through the piano with the same precision and depth as her forms and strategic combat skills, and a gardener who tends the living earth as carefully as she has tended the generations of women who look to her as a model of wisdom and resilience.

Zosia's path has never been the easy one, nor the ordinary one. She trained where few women dared to train, in a time when martial spaces were seldom open to female presence, let alone female mastery. She entered those spaces not for recognition, but for truth — and she carries that truth in her body still, almost seven decades later.

Her life is also a testament to love's endurance and quiet defiance. In marrying her teacher, Zulu — a Marine, a master, and a Black man — she entered into a union that was, at the time, deemed unwelcoming by much of society. Together, they have weathered decades of change, each remaining a steady presence for the other. Their marriage is not only a love story, but a story of resistance, strength, and the breaking of barriers.

Now, in their seventies and eighties, living in Southern California, Zosia and Zulu continue to embody the virtues of the warrior's path: discipline, grace, and integrity. They are a living example of what it means to walk with both fire and compassion, with rootedness and with vision.

This book is not only a reflection of their journey - individually and together - but an offering: to martial artists, women in martial arts, to seekers of discipline and artistry, and to all who strive to live fully in their truth, love, and courage. In these pages, you will hear the voice of a woman who has spent her life carving space where none was offered, who has fought for dignity, for beauty, and for the honor of simply being.

It is my deep privilege to write these words for her. May her story, her strength, and her unwavering spirit reach into you as it has continues to reached into me.

Dr. Michelle Manu, JD, MMsc, PhD, Kumu Po'okela Lua is a 10th Degree Black Belt, Author, Public Speaker, Metaphysician, Media Personality, Elite Athlete

Acknowledgements

To my husband, Chaka Zulu, my life partner, my soul mate, my martial arts teacher, my best friend. You have taught me so much, we have shared so much. Thank you for your loyalty and encouragement.

To Lola, my dear friend, who listened to me at our weekly meetings and provided immeasurable feedback. "Take the audience's hand and walk us there."

To all our Zujitsu[1] Martial Arts Black Belts.
Especially to those senior Black Belts who continue to teach and preserve our Zujitsu legacy—Kenton, Manuel, Doug, Ray, Richard, Eric, Anne, Barry.
You are my dear dojo brothers and sisters.

To my Sister Warriors Tribe, you are the wind beneath my wings.

To my favorite training partner, Lee Goodridge (RIP), you are remembered and missed every day.

---

[1] Zujitsu (also Zujitsu-Ryu) is a synthesis of multiple martial arts founded by Grandmaster Chaka Zulu

Author's Note

This is the story of an interracial couple—me and my husband.

New York, our home city, made interracial marriages legal in 1967, following the Supreme Court decision—on Loving vs. Virginia— that declared all state anti-miscegenation laws were unconstitutional.

California—our home now—was the first state to overturn its ban on interracial marriage in 1948 with the landmark Supreme Court case Perez vs. Sharp.

Chaka and I have been together since 1981, legally married since 1990.

This story is told in three parts.

Part One is my husband's life story up until we met, as told to me when I interviewed him.

Part Two is my life story up until we met.

Part Three is our life together.

What brought us together? What has kept us together? The important role of our devotion to martial arts training. The unique challenges we have faced as an interracial couple.

Contents

Part Three: Our Life Together

If a man does not keep pace with his companions, perhaps it is because he hears a different drummer. Let him step to the music which he hears, however measured or far away.
—Thoreau

Your present circumstances don't determine where you can go; they merely determine where you start.
—Nido Qubein

If you don't like the road you're walking, start paving another one.
—Dolly Parton

Part One

Chaka Zulu

Chapter One

Early Years in Harlem

I was born in Harlem, New York in 1938. At that time, Harlem was very different than it is today. That is where I grew up. Only Black folk lived in Harlem at that time. White folk only visited. Harlem was full of activity with a lot of nightclubs and dancing. White folks would come uptown to intermingle.

We lived in a tenement building on the fifth floor of a walk-up on 8th Avenue, between 134th and 135th Street. My building was between a bar and a pool hall. The bar was cool without much activity except a few drunks. However there were many fights in the pool hall—some of them knife fights. I used to look out the window and watch them beat each other up. My window faced the street and I used to see all sorts of things. I saw a gang called The Chaplains from Brooklyn who used to come up to Harlem to fight our gangs. There were so many gangs at that time. They all tried to get me to join, but I wouldn't join any of them.

Young people didn't have much to do in those days. At one point they had some after school activities in our neighborhood public school, but they closed those schools for no other reason than racism. We used to roller skate, play basketball and ping pong, but they just closed them. There were about four or five schools that were closed, elementary schools and junior high schools.

I lived with my mom and my sister Gloria. My mom had grown up in St. Thomas, United States Virgin Islands (USVI), but moved to New York with several of her siblings. My dad was only there for a short period of my childhood. Then, he had to go into the hospital because of psychological problems—today called severe

PTSD—developed from his time in the Army during World War II. It was also due to the fact that although he was a very bright, intelligent man, he couldn't get a job. He couldn't take care of his family, like many Black veterans at the time. I mean, I found all this out later. I was too young to know all of that at the time. I do remember that he taught me math—he taught me how to add and subtract. That was as far as we got. I didn't see him after that.

My sister was exactly a year younger than me—her birthday just one day before mine. One day a year we were both the same age and she would never let me forget it. That day was always her special day. It was really funny because on that day, she would say, "You can't tell me nothing. I'm the same age as you." We used to like to go to the movies on Saturdays. For a quarter they played several cartoons, a newsreel, a *Mugs Mahoney & the East Side Gang* short, and then one or two main features. We loved this series called *The Jr. G Men*, about these young kids—all White kids —who were like Junior FBI men. They would solve all these mysteries. Once there was a film about Frankenstein and my sister was climbing all over me—scared to death. We would stay in the theater all day because that was what they were doing for the kids in Harlem at the time. There was the RKO Theatre, the Loews Theater and a couple of others I can't recall. Between that and hanging out at the after school centers, that was all we had, until they closed the schools too. Then we had nothing but the streets and gangs.

When we were about six and seven years old, respectively, my mother sent me and my sister to see our grandparents in North Carolina. We were traveling by train alone and we each were wearing a big tag identifying us. We were so little and just scared to death. I remember being picked up at the railroad station in a flatbed truck. We got in with our luggage and as we were heading to the house, we see three Black guys hanging in the trees. I mean, they are hanging by their necks. So now we are really scared and want to go home but we can't go home. We just held on to each other for dear life.

Then (our grandparents) made me kill some chickens. The first one, I had to chop off its head with a hatchet and the second one, I had to wring its neck. I was horrified. Then I remember they took us to a movie theater to see some Black cowboy film. We're sitting in the balcony with all the other Black folks, while the White people are sitting downstairs. Later on, I found out that was because if a fire broke out, all the Blacks could burn up while the Whites escaped. I was just a little boy but instinctively I knew this was wrong.

One of my mother's sisters, Aunt Olivia, lived around the corner from us on 135th Street. She lived by herself after her husband passed away. Aunt Olivia would come over often and take care of me and my sister. I remember one time when—in elementary school—these teachers would find any reason to punish us. Most of them were White, racist and did not want to be teaching in Harlem. There was a Black physical education teacher, a Black female school Principal, and maybe one or two more Black teachers. However, they had no power, no control. All the kids were Black, because no White people lived in Harlem at the time.

So, anytime I did something they thought was wrong, I'd have to hold out my hand, palm up, and it would be beaten with a ruler or one of those pointer sticks. I wouldn't tell my family but my cousin found out and told my Aunt Olivia. My aunt went to the school and told my teacher, "If you ever touch my nephew again you'll never leave Harlem alive. Don't do it again or I'll cut you up with this straight razor like cheese. Don't ever touch him again." It worked. I never got beat again.

I also experienced several unexplainable incidents at a young age. We had a babysitter who watched us while my mother went to work. She had three sons—one who was a good friend of mine. One time we were sitting on their fire escape in the back of the house. I don't remember how it all happened, but I woke up in the hospital. I had fallen down the fire escape to the next landing. I was unconscious so they took me to the hospital. Fortunately, I didn't fall all the way to the ground—just the next landing—because they lived on the fourth floor.

I remember other times, for some reason I was clumsy, or maybe had some unknown neurological issue. I fell down these marble stairs several times and always ended up unconscious. One time I wanted to go to the playground, but when I asked my mother, she was adamant about me not going. I was a jerk and decided to sneak off and go to the playground with my friends, anyway. So I'm in a swing, and the next thing I know, I wake up in the hospital again. I had fallen out of the swing and landed unconscious on the concrete. That used to happen to me all the time. I was never medically diagnosed, but I think it all had an affect on my head.

I was really quiet and timid when I was growing up. I guess the thing that saved me was when I learned how to read. I became a reading fanatic. I had my head in a book all the time. I think part of that was being too scared to face reality. The Marine Corps changed all of that. When I was young, I wanted to be a scientist. I was sent to this school counselor and she told me the only thing I could ever be was an elevator operator.

I was timid, except when it came to protecting my sister. Whenever anything would happen to her, I became an absolute lunatic. There was a guy in our neighborhood named Butchie. All the kids were afraid of him because he was a real bully. One day we were in the school yard, roller skating. My sister went to the drinking fountain and he pushed her head down on the fountain, busting her lip. When I found out about it, I went absolutely crazy. He lived in the next building over from me. So one day when he came out, I had a Pepsi bottle filled with sand and I hit him with it, trying to break every bone in his body. He tried to escape by rolling under a car, but I followed him right under that car. He never bullied another kid in my neighborhood after that experience. From that point on whenever he saw me he would go into panic mode.

Years later, when I was in the Marine Corps, my sister was going out with this guy named Mousie. When I came home on boot camp leave, turns out that Mousie had slapped my sister. When I found out about it, I went around the corner—in uniform—asking for Mousie. Not getting the response I wanted from these guys I just took out my pistol and started firing. I wasn't trying to hit anyone. I just wanted to scare them to death. They scattered, and the next day Mousie came to find me. I had told them that if Mousie (didn't) come to find me "I'm coming after all you guys, so you better send him to me." Well, I slapped the crap out of Mousie, with my hand and with the pistol. I told him, "If you ever put your hands on my sister again I'm coming back. Don't ever touch her again."

There was also an incident with my mother. These guys used to come into our building hallway to gamble. I had no problem with that, but one time my mother called me from the candy store (no cellphones then) to tell me that these guys wouldn't let her in the building. "They're in there gambling and won't let me get upstairs," she said. So I grabbed a baseball bat, went over, and started swinging wildly. Those guys scattered, I scooped up the money, and my mother paid her rent for the next two months. After that they were all so polite and helpful when they saw my mother. Now it was, "Can I help you with your packages?" I realized the only (person) these guys respected was a total lunatic. Nothing else worked, so that's what I became.

Chaka with Mama Drina Gordon

Chapter Two
Reform School

I was a real book worm and mostly a loner. However, I was young and got hooked up with some guys I didn't know anything about and I should have known better. These kids kept encouraging me to get out of the house. When I was about ten or eleven years old, I finally did but started hanging out with the wrong people. This one guy was a real bad influence on the group. We broke into someone's house and robbed him. We were so stupid and so excited about having money, we were just giving it away.

One day this White guy came into the hallway where we lived and he asked me where Mr. G. lived. I said, "Yeah, I'm his son." Well, I got locked up immediately. They called my mother downstairs and she was so upset. Eventually I had to go to court. I went there looking really presentable—all neat and suited up— hoping for the best. The judge was fair and gave me six months at the Warwick School for Boys. The problem with that six month sentence was that every time you had a fight, they would add on a week. I ended up being there quite a bit longer.

The first day I was there, I went to my assigned cottage where we were housed. Boys were separated according to age. The "cottage parents"—a husband and wife who were on staff (and) in charge of the boys in my cottage—asked me if I wanted to "lock." I had no idea what that meant—*what the hell were they talking about?* Turns out, to "lock" means to fight! So they threw me into the shower room and in walks this Puerto Rican guy who was supposed to kick my ass. I was so scared. When the guy threw a punch and hit me, I grabbed him by his throat, slammed his head into the shower nozzle, and just kept slamming. Blood started flying everywhere. When the cottage parents realized what was happening and came in, they couldn't get my hands off his throat— my hand had frozen. They never did that to me again. I was too scared not to fight. These cottage parents were corrupt and out for themselves. The wife was a big, strong woman who would put on black gloves and beat the crap out of anyone she thought was messing up.

After this incident, everyone thought I was crazy—and I was— because I was scared to death. I was out of my mind with fear and that fear turned into serious violence, when necessary. I actually ended up making friends with everyone there. They even let me go bow hunting and I got a pheasant. Everyone had a piece of that pheasant, and it was delicious. I also got a rabbit. I ended up being there about one and a half years, because I wouldn't take anyone's crap. If anyone tried to bully me, there would be a fight. It was as simple as that because I was too scared not to fight. That's how my six months turned into about eighteen months.

I remember when we used to march to chow, the counselors would call cadence, and would make each boy call cadence too. When my time came, I called the cadence and those guys were marching just like Marines. I was singing that damn cadence and they were strutting. I think what clinched my relationship with the older guys was that Floyd Patterson's son was in there and he was a bully. He tried to bully me, but it didn't work!

Chapter Three
The U.S. Marine Corps, 1956-1962

When I finally got out and went back to Harlem, I started training in Judo at the Harlem YMCA. I had tried boxing when I was younger but that didn't sit well with me. The glove thing felt strange but at the time, that was all that was available. However, Judo felt right and I was a brown belt by the time I went into the Marines at seventeen. When (I was) in the Marine Corps, I met a gentleman who was a 2nd degree Black Belt in Judo. He and I eventually became the Company Judo Instructors. It was fun and I learned a lot from him. Eventually, I went into Marine Corps Force Recon—the elite MC unit where I started studying Tae Kwon Do with some crazy Korean Marines—and got my Black Belt.

I will never forget what inspired me to join the U.S. Marine Corps. One day, I was on 5th Avenue and 34th Street. I saw this Marine walking down the street. He was so sharp—everybody was stopping to look at this guy. He was the sharpest looking m-fker I had ever seen in my life, and he knew it. I said to myself, "That's what I want to be." He didn't just walk down the street, he marched down the street, and everybody got out of his way. He was tall, obviously in shape, and just magnificent. I'll never forget him. I wanted to be a Marine, not only because he was sharp, but because that denoted absolute discipline, although I didn't realize it at the time. I think being involved in Judo at the time, was focusing my mind on self discipline. I was about fifteen or sixteen at the time. I asked my mother if I could join the Marines, but she said I had to wait until I was seventeen.

"Once A Marine, Always, A Marine"

The Marine corps helped shape my attitude about not giving up, finishing a job, loyalty, honesty—all those things. Besides the physical aspects, I think those are the things that have stuck with me and are what I transfer into my martial arts and into my students. I think the biggest thing is *attitude*.

I joined the U.S. Marine Corps when I turned seventeen. I went to boot camp at Parris Island in South Carolina. Right before I arrived, a guy named Sergeant McKeon had taken a platoon out at night and marched them through the swamp. Seven of them had drowned. As the newest platoon, we had to go search for the bodies. *Welcome to the Marines!*

I don't know if it was racially motivated or not but the Black guys seemed to get beaten often for all kinds of stupid reasons and they called it *training*. Many of the towns we went to only allowed Black Marines in certain areas. I didn't feel like the Marine Corps was supporting us. When we finally graduated Boot Camp and had liberty, the nearby town was called Jacksonville—about five miles from the base. The Marines had a contract with Trailway Bus Line, and they would come to the base to pick us up to go to town. The Black Marines would have to stand outside the bus until the seats were filled with the White Marines. Then the Black Marines could stand up the five miles to town.

Then in town, we had a certain section across the tracks where we had to go. There was a huge Black guy called Tiny who had a long nightstick he was supposed to use to control us. I don't know why, because we weren't out of control. One night, there was some kind of altercation and he came up to me with his nightstick like he was going to hit me. I told him "go right ahead" but you better kill me, because I'm coming back. He backed off, because he knew I was serious.

While in the Marines, in uniform—traveling with other White Marines—I often couldn't get out of the car because they wouldn't serve me in the restaurant, unless I went to the back door. I had to use the "colored" restroom. I remember a sign in the window in Virginia. It said, "Nigger, if you can read, run. If you can't read, run anyway." And I'm supposed to be a U.S. Marine *defending who?!* No man, I learned my lesson real quick.

After boot camp, I was stationed on Vieques Island in Puerto Rico where we trained and did maneuvers with the Navy at the Naval Training Range. There was a town nearby called Isabel Segunda. We were told not to go to this town because the people were hostile to Marines and they would *chop you up* with machetes and leave your body in front of the base. I understood it immediately. The Marines were a lot of White guys who thought they were privileged and treated the locals poorly, without respect. I said, "F-k this, I'm going to town." We were told definitely don't (go) to The Canyon in town. Well, as soon as I got a chance, I went down to The Canyon. I knocked on a door and in my broken Spanish, I spoke to this family. I told them I was a Marine who just wanted a home cooked meal and was willing to pay for it. They accepted me right away and even offered me their beautiful daughter. I stayed with them—off and on—for three nights. I was the only Marine who could go down to The Canyon without getting hurt.

But one night, I went down with this other Black guy who was from Ohio. He had blond hair and blue eyes. He was a lunatic that I met because we almost had a fight, but instead became friends. So, we went to Isabel Segunda together. There were a bunch of other Marines and Sailors in town who weren't supposed to be there—all AWOL. Here we are and then the military police show up and everybody starts running and yelling "Polizia, Polizia." So, we started running, too. I started running down this dirt road and I'm running my ass off. There's a police vehicle behind (me), chasing me. Then, somebody started firing pistols. Well, there was a barbed wire fence on either side of the road. I ran right through this fence and I don't know why it didn't chop me into shreds. So, now I'm running through this field and there's a shed. Just about as I'm going to pass this shed, a cow steps out in front of me. I hit this cow a shot with a punch—*boom*—and my hand blows up like a basketball. I'm still running and now crying and the police are still chasing me. Well, I ended up in Marine lock-up. In Vieques, lock-up was a round enclosure surrounded by barbed wire and you were given a task. My task was to break big rocks into little rocks with a sledge hammer. I spent three days in lock-up, eating only "Piss & Punk" which was bread and water with a pinch of salt.

On another occasion, my buddy and I went into town to have a drink and hang out. As we are about to enter this bar/nightclub, we open the door and there's a big fight going on. Everyone is swinging and throwing bottles and chairs. My friend and I look at each other and say *let's back out of this place*. This is not what we want. However, as we're backing out of the door, we turn around and who's standing there in front of us? A whole squad of military police officers. We're trying to explain to them that we have nothing to do with it, but they weren't having it. So we said, "F-k it, let's fight." We rushed back in and started kicking and punching, as the MP's came in, beating the crap out of everyone with their night sticks. The next morning when I woke up I was in a barbed wire enclosure, given a sledgehammer, and told to bust those big rocks into little rocks—again! But we were wronged that time because we had nothing to do with that fight. Unfortunately, that's not how the MP's saw it.

There was a guy named Lieutenant Joyce who was our platoon leader. He was a super nice guy who really liked me, even though I would kid around with him all the time. One day, we were getting ready to go do Net Training. This is where they hang a huge cargo net on the side of the ship and the troops have to climb up and down this net with all their gear. It's dangerous because the net is attached to the ship and attached to a steel landing craft that slams along the ship. If you get caught between them, or slip and fall, you've got a problem! So we're on the beach preparing to go on the landing craft to the ship. Lt. Joyce gets up on a sand dune, puts his hands on his hips and yells "If you want to be f-king Marines you gotta be tough. You gotta be a bad ass." I mean, he went through the whole deal. It was hysterical, because the moment we got on the ship he turned green and started puking everywhere. I never let him live it down either. He was one of the good guys.

Marines were Marines and fights would break out when we went to most of the towns. When some of these guys fought they had straight razors. One time in Greenville, North Carolina, I was with six other Marines. We went to this nightclub that was in a corrugated hut. They had a juke box, a bar and booths with seats. We went in, just looking to have a good time. Since we were Marines in uniforms, the ladies start gravitating towards us, immediately. A while later, the door opens and in walks all of these local Black guys. They gather by the juke box, talking to each other but they're looking at us. I'm saying, *uh-oh, this is going to present us with a problem because they think we're taking their women.* So I told my guys, "There's only seven of us and there's a whole lot more of them—maybe fifteen or sixteen—and it's time for us to get out of here." We left and jumped into the car to take off. As we're pulling away, these guys came out of the bar with pistols and started firing at us. We got out of there fast, but we came back. We came back a couple of nights later and we had all kinds of weapons with us. I brought some tear gas grenades. I opened the door, threw one in and slammed the door shut. Everybody started choking and gagging—rushing out. We started open firing on them, we didn't hit anyone, we were just trying to scare them to death. We had done nothing wrong and they messed with the wrong guys.

I had another friend whom I had known before the service. He was a big, muscular guy from Long Island, New York. He and I got into a lot of trouble for dunking a guy off the ship. We were laying up on the hatch getting some sun and fresh air. Down in the ship the diesel oil fumes made everyone puke. So this sailor—a ship police officer—comes up and yells at us to get off the hatch and get down below. We said *okay* but he walked off and we didn't move. A few minutes later he comes back and yells, "I thought I told you Niggers to go below." *Uh-Oh!* He messed up, said the magic word! I gave the guy my fist and then we both wrapped a rope around his ankles, and started dipping his head into the ocean.

Unfortunately they caught us and we ended up in lock up, eating Piss & Punk. The security officers would mess with us, too. They would come in the middle of the night, throw a bucket of water in the cell and yell that the ship was sinking. Meanwhile, we're locked in the cell, asleep and freaking out. It wasn't funny then, but it sure is funny now.

There was this other guy—a fella from North Carolina—a big tobacco chewing redneck, and he didn't like Niggers or Jews. One night, my Jewish friend and I were talking in the bunkhouse. So this guy yells, "You Niggers. You better shut the f-k up or I'll come over and kick your ass." So we get real quiet but that night I waited until I heard him snoring and snuck out of my bunk. We had these mops with super thick handles. I took that handle off the mop and started beating this guy. He couldn't get out of his bed because, in the Marines, they make you tuck in those sheets real tight. I beat the crap out of him, in the dark. The next day he was messed up but nobody ever told him that I did it because they all hated him. They ended up transferring him out.

One day I'm on Mess Duty, as the senior guy, and I thought I was hot stuff. Stupid, hot stupid is what I was! This White guy comes early and instead of me politely telling him that he was early, I went into macho mode and started talking all this dumb stuff. As I'm talking, one of my platoon brothers walks in to overhear the conversation. Meanwhile, this White guy says back to me, very quietly, "I'll meet you behind the mess hall at 6 o'clock." My response, "Okay m-f-ker I'll be there." The clincher was, my friend who had overheard all this says, "Do you know who this guy is? He's a brown belt in Shorin Ryu Karate." As soon as he said that, my heart fell to my knees. *Oh, crap!* I might know a whole lot of judo but this guy knows karate. In those days, karate was this mystical thing to be feared—not common, like now. So, I'm trying to figure out how to get out of this mess, because I realized this guy is going to punish me! I decided to humble myself. I gave him extra pie and started apologizing like crazy. We eventually became friends and I learned a lesson!

There was another situation when we were on maneuvers. I always woke up earlier than everyone else. I was used to early mess duty and used to go jogging before that, so I wouldn't gain weight and (would) stay in shape. We're all in these little two man tents. I wake up early and see all these guys, the aggressors, coming through the bushes. They're sneaking up and I'm the only one awake. I see the flame throwers that would only fire water when on maneuvers but it would come out with such force (it could) knock you down. So, as they're coming up, I start spraying them with the water from the flame thrower, knocking them down 'till it was empty. Then, I see this guy coming towards me and I pulled out my Bowie knife. Something had snapped in my head and I forgot I wasn't in combat. I went towards this guy—a big tall White guy— and he said to me in this soft voice, "That ain't necessary. Why do you need that?" I looked at him and thought he was a damn angel with a halo around his head. I put the knife back and became silent. He actually scared me with his soft voice and that glow around his body. I can still visualize it now. By that time, everyone had woken up and heard the commotion. Maneuvers were so realistic that they could easily be confused with real combat.

On one occasion on maneuvers, we were the aggressors for this Ohio State Reserve Marine Battalion. Again, we were supposed to simulate combat conditions. Well, somehow I got captured by them. They made me march with them, carrying one of their machine guns. However, the moment they blinked their eyes, the machine gun and I were gone! They couldn't believe it. I actually got a commendation for that action. I remember they would be marching down the road and we would snatch them, covering their mouths and make them disappear. One guy we tied to a tree, beat him with cactuses and put snakes (non-venomous) in his pocket. One night it took me a half an hour or more to crawl into their camp. I finally snuck in and this guy was fast asleep in a hammock. Now we've got all this green and black smeared over our camouflage faces and camouflage uniforms. We looked like a bunch of bushes. So I crawled over to this guy, I tapped him and put my finger to my lips for him to be quiet. He didn't say anything because he was scared to death. I mean, I'm not only a Marine, but I'm a Black Marine! He got down out of his bunk, I put my knife around him and crawled his ass right out of there. I got a commendation for that action, too.

Another time, on maneuvers, I was sent out to be "the point." His job is to go ahead, see if there are any enemy troops around, and if so, he'll probably be the first one killed. We're all walking through this really thick jungle-like forest and I'm looking around. It's pitch black and I'm already scared to death. The trail is super narrow and just then I glance towards a bush and see these eyes looking at me. There's a face behind the eyes, but I can only see the eyes. I spun around and opened fire. Fortunately for him, the weapons we were using had blanks. My platoon comes rushing up to me, I'm freaking out, and my corporal is telling me to *calm down*. I told him what happened. That was the first and last time I was ever "the point!"

I also went on maneuvers in the jungles of Panama. We were training with the army at that time. We stopped for a break and there was a big log, a felled tree. So I went to sit on this tree. On this tree was a big stump. I didn't think anything of it, until the stump moved! Turns out what I thought was a stump was a huge spider. Boy, I almost ran out of Panama (laughing out loud).

Panama was wild. One of my Marine Corps buddies was an Italian guy named Tony. He was a big dude. He laid his poncho out in this jungle path for the night. Next thing we know, he starts screaming. We had flashlights but we weren't allowed to turn them on. But we said *hell with that* and turned them on. Unfortunately,

Tony had lain his poncho on an ant hill and they were carrying him away, literally! We were laughing ourselves sick.

We had this big, Black guy from North Carolina who was a Corporal. It was pitch black and he bellowed out, "Oh shit, something just crawled across my foot and it took two minutes to cross." Everyone started turning on (their) flashlights. Well there were snakes everywhere. You talk about some tough ass Marines running and scrambling, trying to get the heck out of there.

The Marines had these vehicles, big steel machines that they put the troops in. They had tracks and would swim across the water. We were told that if it sunk, we would have to sit there until it was completely filled with water so that the water pressure would be even. Only then would we be able to open the hatch and swim out. We would be swimming out with all this gear, packs and cartridge belts, helmets and rifles, swimming up to the surface. I believe several Marines drowned in a maneuver like this one because the hatch wouldn't open.

Maneuvers can definitely be dangerous. I remember when we were supposed to perform a demonstration for some Spanish Marine Generals. We had practiced these maneuvers for at least two weeks. My job was to run into this firing bunker, throw in a one pound charge of TNT, and get out. I had been doing it for weeks and had it down pat. However, the day of the demo, it went totally wrong. I went in like I was supposed to do and threw in my one pound stick. Then, when I turned around and went to get out of the hole, all this shale was on the ground. So every step I took to get out, I would slide back down. I never got out of the hole. The TNT went off and I went flying out of the hole. I woke up in the hospital, totally banged up and for a few minutes, I could't even remember who I was. I'm surprised I even lived.

Then there was Escape and Evasion school where they treated you just like you were a POW (prisoner of war). They would beat you, pour water on you, do all kinds of things. Your objective was to escape. Your main obligation was not to give them any information—just your service number, rank and name, and that was it. I don't remember being there longer than three days and I was out of there. Many complaints were issued by officers from different branches of the service who had to go through the training but were unable to escape. They complained it was too rough but no—it wasn't too rough compared to what would happen if you were really captured. Yes, it was rough, and it should have been rough, otherwise *why do it*! It taught me a lot.

USMC Chaka

Chapter Four

Losing My Sister

By 1961, my sister Gloria had gotten married and had two young children. While on leave, I heard that her husband had hit her with a stick. As I was about to go to Brooklyn to their house, my mother caught me jumping in a cab. When I told her what happened, she got in the cab with me. When we arrived, her husband acted all arrogant and self righteous. I was silent, afraid that if I started I would go ballistic. My mother tried to talk to him, but he continued with his messed up attitude. I didn't say another word, I went in the kitchen, got a huge knife and threw it on the bed. I told him to reach for it. He looked at me, then at the knife, and started to panic. I'm looking *death* at him now, and just waiting for him to go for it, but he didn't. We got ready to leave. I was walking out, holding the younger baby (the older one was with a neighbor). My mother was walking behind me with my sister. Then I heard my sister say, "Oh here he comes." Next, I hear shots fired. I turned around and saw my sister drop immediately and my mother run behind a car. I saw him firing at my mother. I put the baby in the grass and started running towards him. He saw me coming, turned and fled. My sister lay dead.

The rest of that day is a blur. I was so enraged, I came back to Manhattan to get a pistol because I was going back to kill him and his whole family. My friend—who I went to get the pistol from—owned the candy store where I used to hang out. The moment he saw the look on my face, he had a pistol but he wouldn't give it to me. Eventually, however, when I went to court for (my sister's husband's) trial, I had a pistol with me. In those days, there were no metal detectors and I had snuck one into the courthouse. I was just sitting in court, waiting for them to bring him out. My mother realized I had the gun and she told Detective O'Connor. He came over to me and started talking in this soft voice, calmed me down and talked me into giving him the pistol. I was still going to kill him with my bare hands. They decided not to bring him into court to avoid a confrontation, seeing my determination. He went to prison, I'm not sure for how long. He did not get the life sentence (or worse) that he deserved. My mother kept up with it but would never tell me his whereabouts, as she knew I would seek revenge.

The Marine Corps was wonderful and I enjoyed the hell out of it, afterwards. I was crazy then, I just didn't give a f-k. I didn't think I was going to live past twenty, anyway. I was out of my head. I was Black and I had seen enough about racism to know I'm not going to survive this because I'm not going to take anybody's bullsh*t. The combat side of my time in the Marines has been purposefully left out. It is not something I have spoken about to anyone and shall remain so.

Gloria, Chaka's Sister

Chapter Five
1960's Civil Rights Movement

When I came out of the Marine Corps in 1962, I was trying to decide what I wanted to do in life. I needed a job, so I went to work for the Pinkerton Detective Agency. It was the largest security agency in New York at the time. One of my assignments was in a New Jersey electronics plant. I went undercover as the maintenance man to try to find out who was stealing. By the time I found out, they discovered my identity, too. I was on the phone with my supervisor in one of the old fashioned phone booths when these guys approached. I had just enough time to stick the broom handle in the door to keep it closed. They were trying to get me and a couple (of them) had knives. Fortunately, my supervisor had called the State Troopers who arrived and I was fine. However, that taught me a good lesson. My martial arts changed from that point on, instantly. The realization hit me that with all my judo and tae kwon do, it wasn't going to work in that phone booth. So, ever since that day, my martial arts has been changing continuously, and always will continue to evolve.

During that time, I was invited to Fire Island by friends and students who had timeshares there. I remember that I was only one of two Black guys on the island. The other guy was a horse trainer for some wealthy guy. My first day there, I worked out on the beach for hours. Later on, I had been invited to one of the night clubs for a few beers and some dancing. I was a little shy, so I sat nursing a beer, watching people enjoy themselves. As I was sitting, a couple came and sat at a table slightly at an angle in front of me so I could see them, clearly. At one point, they got up to go on the dance floor and the woman laid her purse on the back of her chair. A short while later a woman walked into the club and looked around. She walked past the table with the purse on the chair, snatched it up and went to the ladies room. A short time after she came out empty handed and walked out the door. When the couple came back to their seat, the woman noticed her bag was gone. They approached me and questioned me and I explained to them what I saw happen. They called the police who also questioned me, but I showed them my Pinkerton Detective Agency identification so I was not held. In any case, the last ferry boat had left the island and wouldn't return until the next day. By then, I was seriously pissed off and figured that since this woman was so successful, she would return to try it again.

Sure enough, as I stood there waiting for the noon ferry the next day, she came walking down the gangway without a care in the world. Of course, until I grabbed her by the back of her neck and told her in no uncertain terms that if she tried to fight, pull away or pull a knife, I would break every bone in her body. The look on my face told her everything. I marched her right to the police station where she confessed and was booked. After that, I could do no wrong on the Island. When the story got around, I could get in any club without paying, although I detected an ulterior motive. *Who would not want a free bouncer or body guard hanging around their place?* Most of them had already seen my skills when at the beach. Even the police patrol would come down to the beach and see me working out. Although nunchakus were supposedly not allowed, they would just watch me without saying a word. They had become my friends. I felt they trusted me and would likely appreciate my help, if a situation arose.

When General Douglas MacArthur came to New York City, I was among the staff assigned by the Pinkerton Agency to be in his security detail. As Chairman of the Sperry Rand Corporation,

MacArthur was in town to discuss some top secret information. The meeting was held at a well known hotel in Manhattan and absolutely no cameras were allowed. We were outside of the conference room when all these guys with cameras come rushing toward us. I put my hands up to stop them. Well, this one guy decides to put his hand in my face and push it back. I couldn't believe somebody would do that to me. I went absolutely nuts. I couldn't control myself and I broke up some cameras that day. A couple of days later, I was called into the Pinkerton office to explain myself. They were not on board with my explanation. I told the boss, "Let me tell you something. You put your hand in my face and I'll kick your ass, too. Simple as that. So do what you gotta do." In those days, I just didn't care about getting fired or none of that stuff. *You're going to respect me*, period or I'm out of there. My boss said I could leave, so I did, for good. It wasn't the first time I had been disrespected on this job but it was the last.

At that time, I was really into judo. I had one student named Charles Turner. He was my first green belt. We used to work out every chance we would get. We trained at the St. Phillips Community Center on 133rd Street. We were in a room at the top, that had some mats. Sadly, he went to Mexico and was stabbed to death. I also taught judo at the Morningside Community Center.

I remember being involved with a protest because they weren't teaching African American History in the public schools. A whole group of people claimed they would be there in the morning to protest, but come the next day, most of those people flaked out. There were just a few of us confronting a whole bunch of cops. These cops surrounded us, acting real aggressive. So we got back to back and said "F-k it, let's fight!" They had no idea that I was a former Marine and judo instructor. Cops were flying everywhere because my judo was taking over. I was punching, kicking and throwing—dropping them left and right. That's when Lee, wife of Ed Bell (RIP), was watching out the window. I didn't even know she was looking. Bell was a Professor at William Paterson College, a black belt (who) became a good friend and student. The only thing that saved me was a woman who jumped in front of a cop, who was going to shoot me in the back. He stopped and holstered it instead. I didn't know about this until later.

They couldn't control me at all. I was a wild man. Finally, this one officer, a captain I knew from a previous situation, said to me in a pleading voice, "Zulu, please stop." I looked at him and I just stopped. I told him I stopped because of the way he asked me but I said *no one is going to put me in handcuffs*. So this one cop comes up as I'm about to get in the police car and he screams, "Cuff him!" And I went ballistic again and hit this guy a shot, knocked him flat-out. I was about to stomp on his neck when the same captain asked me to stop again. So I stopped and got into the police car. They took me and four other guys to the precinct on 135th Street. They put us in this room, sitting and waiting. All of a sudden, the door opens. In walks a group of White cops wrapping the thongs of their nightsticks around their wrists because they're going to beat us. I jumped up and said, "Let's fight these guys. They're going to beat us anyway." I had a long, steel hatpin in the seam of my pants that they never found when they searched me. One of them saw me slide it out and said, "He's got something in his hand." I told him to come and find out what it is. By that time I was calm—I was ready to die. However, just before the fight breaks out, the door opens again. This time it's five or six Black police officers. I even knew a couple of them because we had trained together. They told the White cops, "It's not going to happen on (their) watch. They put their hands on their pistols. The White cops backed down. Later, my good friend Ben Yusef, walked into the precinct with an attaché case. He was all suited up, told them that he was my attorney and walked me out of there. I don't know how he pulled that off. He had been in WWII and Korea and he was upset about the overt racism, too. He was crazier than me and just didn't care.

One day, Martin Luther King came to town. However, the people I hung out with were in total opposition to his movement for integration. There was a famous church in Harlem where he was going to speak and we decided we would go. We wouldn't interrupt anything but we would go there to let him know that we were in total opposition to integration. About thirty of us got all dressed up in black suits, white shirts and black ties. We went and sat in the first four or five front rows and just sat there. We never said a word. Just sat there, stoic, pissed off but we weren't going to cause any disruptions. After it was over, we marched out and that was the end of it. He got the message. Malcolm (X) was not with us then—he was with the Nation of Islam. When I was working for Malcolm, he had left the Nation of Islam and was on his own.

I was really radical in those days. I was pissed off a lot. I knew quite a few guys who probably should have been behind bars. I had a great relationship with a guy named Bumpy Johnson. Everyone knew him because he had been in several prisons, including Sing Sing and Alcatraz. The authorities accused him of killing about seven people but they couldn't prove it. So, they couldn't keep him incarcerated. He and I were good friends. There was another guy who was my friend. I had no idea at the time but he was the head of *Harlem's Murder, Inc.* He was one sharp dude—a little thin, sharp dresser. A great guy who you would never suspect would be doing that kind of stuff.

We had a congressman named Adam Clayton Powell, who represented Harlem in the House of Representatives. He used to hang out at this Harlem bar with his bodyguards. One evening, seven or eight of us went down to this bar, confronted his bodyguards, and disarmed them. We told Powell, if you take any elective office and don't do the right thing, we will be coming to see you. And we won't be coming *friendly*. Anything you do will be affecting our lives, so behave accordingly or we will be back. We were determined to fight for our rights.

**Chaka Zulu Performing at a
Martial Arts Tournament**

Chapter Six
Receiving My True Name

The year 1964 was also an important year for me, personally. Chaka Zulu is not my given name. It was given to me by the Zulu tribe. I consider my "given name" to be my slave name. At the time, I was teaching African Dance with my first wife. I met the tribe when I was doing a demonstration at the 1964 World's Fair in Queens, New York. I danced with them for awhile and they gave me the name. We went through a serious ritual and I've been Chaka Zulu ever since—and will be until I die. It's a powerful name and I consider myself powerful. I guess to be called Chaka Zulu you have to be powerful. I was named after Shaka (with an "S") Zulu—the King of the Zulus—who built a tribe of thirty people, into thousands. He taught some warrior techniques that no one at the time knew and he incorporated a lot of different tribes into one. That's who I feel I am, who I feel I'm descended from, even though I can't prove it. I feel it inside—that's enough for me. And the power that it gives me, I don't know anything else.

Chapter Seven
Leading the Youth

I had a great relationship with the neighborhood kids and used to take them camping. I had been a boy scout and loved that stuff. We used to go deep into New Jersey and have a great time. One day there was a meeting at the 69th Armory with a few hundred kids. They were asked who they could relate to in the community and my name came up. That's when I got hired to work at (the) HARYOU-ACT.

From the NYC Department of Records and Information Services:

"Dr. Kenneth B. Clark, a psychology professor, founded the HARYOU organization in 1962, along with several ministers, community leaders, and government officials. HARYOU argued that an important step in delinquency prevention was to empower Black youth by creating more job opportunities, providing job training, and assisting delinquent youths in rehabilitation. In addition to disseminating funds, HARYOU sought to increase Black consciousness and pride. In the midst of the Civil Rights Movement and the Harlem Riots, their mission became extraordinarily relevant...HARYOU-ACT received $3.4 million from (New York) City and $1 million from the federal government to administer these programs."

Unfortunately, as evidenced by a documented comic strip, "School officials don't seem to want to do anything for our kids. As far as they're concerned, our children are hopeless."

I was given the job of Community Organizer. I began by approaching all the neighborhood landlords, asking them for the use of their basements for youth activities. I set up mini movie theaters, services to assist elders with grocery shopping, an African fashion station where girls could design and sew clothes, an art studio, a library, babysitting services, and homework help. We did several parades, including a big parade at the World's Fair in Queens, New York. I walked in with this huge umbrella over my head in my African costume, my wife next to me. All the men and women were behind us, in their African costumes and we performed African dances. In fact, that's where I met Moses Powell. He was doing a demo with his students.

At one point, I was the HARYOU Brigadier General of Cadets. I had over two-hundred kids—good kids—who just needed some direction. Since I was a Marine, I decided to make these kids Marines. I convinced the people in charge to buy them camouflage uniforms and fake rifles. I had them marching all over the armory and they loved it. They really appreciated the discipline and direction.

I also remember one time, the kids were supposed to be paid a stipend, but the money was being withheld. At the time, there were a few hundred teenagers who were pissed off and fed up with this society and so they turned to Islam. They called themselves the Five Percenters because they were the five percent of the Muslims who smoked and drank. They were referred to as a gang (Wikipedia). They scared many White teachers out of Harlem. They were known to knife them and I think one teacher was killed. Everyone was scared of these dangerous kids.

So on this (one) day, all of these kids are packed into this hall, and the White staff running the organization wants to send me into this chaos to calm them all down. I go in and I'm talking to them but their rhetoric is harsh and they're talking themselves into a big problem. I'm standing in the middle of them all trying to calm them down and explain what's happening with their checks. Fortunately for me, one of them was a really tall guy whom I knew and he started telling them, "Hey, don't f-k with this guy. I've been telling you all about him. This is Zulu. He will kill half of you before you can even blink an eye."

Now all of them are looking at me, differently. I can see the respect. I told them I wasn't sure what was going on but I was going to find out. I said I would get their checks—they would get their money. Now I was pissed off, too! So, I went to the YMCA on 135th Street—where the HARYOU project had office space—to talk to the comptroller, this White woman who controls the paychecks. I'm telling her what's going on, that she needs to come up with a solution because these kids are going to get wild and I won't be able to control them. Well, she starts an argument with me and then threatens to "sic the Five Percenters on me." I was outraged. *She's going to sic Black people on me?! To hurt me!* I lost it. I said, "Just wait until I come back. These kids are going to get paid or you're not leaving here."

I went to my stash in St. Nicholas Park, got a fragmentation hand grenade, went back to her office, slammed the door and locked it. I said nobody is leaving until everybody gets paid. I was suicidal by that time. I couldn't believe she was going to sic Black people on me, to hurt me. When they all realized how crazy I was getting, everyone got paid. The next day, Armando, a Muslim friend of mine who was a serious martial artist with huge knuckles that make mine look like green peas, went to the office with a sawed off shotgun. He told them the next time Zulu has a problem with any of you, "I'm coming back". They all knew who he was and greatly feared him. I had no problems after that incident.

The program was a great success and growing, until the stupidity started. The people in charge thought I was building some political base and began giving me lots of grief. It got to the point that if I didn't give the word, these kids wouldn't function because they liked and respected me. Eventually the harassment by the higher ups just got to be too much for me, so I left.

Chaka Teaching the Youth

Chapter Eight

Working with the Establishment

I was living in Harlem, married to my first wife, with a young daughter, working as the manager of the Truth Coffee Shop. It was located on Seventh Avenue between 134th and 135th Streets. Many of the so-called radicals of that time hung out there. Some of them were Stokely Carmichael, Angela Davis, Malcolm X, Louis Farrakan, and Leroy Jones. They would all come to the coffee shop and have discussions. A lot of revolutionary thinking emanated from that coffee shop. It was across the street from Small's Paradise, owned by Wilt Chamberlain. That club had a lot of partying and dancing in that place.

I had quite a few different jobs during this time. One of my jobs was working at the Bronx Criminal Courthouse. I used to take *working parties* out. These guys were all prisoners with *liberty cards*. They were convicts but not violent offenders. I had to take them out around The Bronx to stores and other places to clean. I told all of these guys that if anyone steals anything out of these stores while on my watch, "You'll have a problem you won't be able to handle." Turns out one of the guys, Big John Slaughter, knew me from before.

Apparently, the first day I walked in, these convicts started giggling because I was in a suit and tie. I didn't know any better, but I said I'd tear this suit off my back "kicking the sh't out of you guys". Then Big John got up and said he knew me and I was no one to mess with. So, I got their attention and respect. If any one of these guys tried to steal something, the rest would snatch him and stop it immediately. I had told them "if one guy steals anything, everyone will pay for it." I had the best work parties.

Later on, I had a problem with the boss lady. One afternoon, some big Black guy came into the office, all pissed off and started yelling and screaming at the secretary. I could see she was in a panic and didn't know what to do. I was sitting at my desk in my office listening to it all. Then, I walked out and said to him, "Who are you talking to? You better sit the hell down or I'll put my foot deep into your ass!" So, he calmed down and started being polite. About an hour later, my boss calls me into her office and says to me, "Zulu, do you like your job? You can't talk to the clients like that!" *What??* I said, "This guy was threatening the secretary and she was frightened to death. What was she supposed to do? What would have happened if I wasn't there?" (My boss) just kept on with her nonsense and I quit.

There was this guy who thought he was a Black Nationalist but was being misled. I forget his name. Turned out he and another guy tried to rob a bank and they got caught. When the police interviewed him, for some unknown reason, he had named me as involved. However, when the police investigated they realized I had nothing to do with it. So, one day I'm at the Coffee Shop with my daughter and someone comes in to tell me this guy who involved me in the bank heist is around the corner at the YMCA. I lost it. I asked someone to watch my kid till I got back and I ran to the "Y". I caught this guy in the hallway and I slammed him against the wall. Then, I pulled out my pistol and drove it into his mouth. I said, "I'll put a bullet into your head, you involve me with a bank robbery, something with which I had no involvement!" So he's shaking, his hands are up, my pistol is in his mouth, and I'm in a rage. I'm about to lose it. Fortunately, the doors flew open and these people saw me there with my gun in his mouth. I realized I couldn't kill him in front of them, so I snatched it out of his mouth, put it in my pocket, and stormed out. I went back to the coffee shop and never saw him again.

After a while things started changing. When Malcolm broke up with Elijah Mohammed, it got bad—people threatening each other and stuff. I remember these guys came into the coffee shop, threatening me and my friend because they wanted us to join their group. We both had our pistols under the table, pointed at their groin, and they didn't even realize it. *The crap I had to go through.* I had to carry a pistol all the time. I never liked it—it wasn't my thing. I didn't like pistols, rifles, none of that, even though I was a Marine.

In those days, there was a lot of segregation. Police brutality was common. The police would sic dogs on Black people and spray them with fire hoses. There were those of us who wouldn't accept it. So when we had those encounters, rather than submit like the Martin Luther King followers, we wouldn't—we would fight. Some of us got injured, and others got killed.

There's something about me that's a little different than other people. During that time, I was feisty and intense. Many people were attracted to me, then because there was a lot of Civil Rights (activity) happening, much racism and I just wouldn't accept any of it. I was a little crazy, then and prone to violence. After all, I was a Marine—*Once A Marine, Always A Marine*—who fought for my country and was still being treated like a slave. Everything that pertained to Civil Rights that I was involved in, all had to do with what was being done to me. Not me as an individual but my people —my Black people. Violence surrounded me.

Chapter Nine

Leaving Harlem for Greenwich Village

There were a few reasons that made me decide to leave Harlem for Greenwich Village. My wife and I had separated and Harlem was seeing more violence. One day, there was a gang fight on my block, shots were fired and a slug came through my mother's window. That started me thinking about living somewhere else. Then, finally, my apartment was robbed. I mean, they totally cleaned me out. "They" meaning other Black folk because no White people would dare come up to rob anyone in Harlem. I decided it was time to leave.

A friend of mine was working as Chief of Security in the East Village but was leaving his job to open his own security and private investigation agency. He offered me the job and I accepted. The place was called Electric Circus on St. Marks Place. "The Electric Circus nightclub was a multi-media extravaganza that invited guests to play games, dress as you like, dance, sit, think, tune in and turn on. An East Village fixture from 1967-71, the club featured circus performers and light shows sandwiched between some obscure acts like The Velvet Underground, The Grateful Dead, Sly and the Family Stone, The Allman Brothers, The Doors and Santana." archives.sva.edu

I had twenty guys working under me. As one of the club attractions, the security personnel wore bell bottom pants, white karate gi (uniform) tops, and a black belt from whatever system in which they trained. On the top floor attic, my predecessor had brought in large mats and a ring where new security prospects were tested on their skills. They also had to pass an interview regarding their attitude and ability to follow the rules. Since mostly teenagers frequented the club, it was important to protect them and avoid violence. I had a policy, if you have to hit somebody, don't hit them in the face where bruising would show—just hit them on their body. However, we are not policemen and I didn't want them beating up on people because at 4:30 a.m., we still had to go home. Those who could not abide by the rules were terminated.

I had hired a black belt I knew—Louis Delgado—as security at the Electric Circus. I explained the rules to him on how to handle unruly customers. One evening while on patrol, Louis came across a guy blatantly smoking a joint. He forcibly bum-rushed the guy out of the building, pushing and shoving him, unnecessarily. The guy stopped and asked Louis not to push him because he would leave peaceably. This was one of the rules that Delgado did not follow—"do not abuse your authority." It turns out "that guy" was a biker from Brooklyn. At the end of the night when we had to close up and go home, as we stepped outside, there were at least thirty or more bikers waiting for us. Fortunately for us, we had the support of the bouncers from the Dom (a popular bar) downstairs, too. It looked like we were going to have to fight these guys. Meanwhile, Bob Chin, our Chinese black belt had gone back into the building to make a phone call. A short while later, entering from either end of the block, were at least a hundred young Chinese men walking slowing towards everyone, some carrying very unusual weapons. Realizing this might turn into a blood bath, somehow, Ronald Tagonashi and I were able to talk down the situation and deescalate it before any violence erupted. This was an eye opener for my entire security team as to why I had made these rules of conduct. I was still a Marine!

One night, one of my guys—who was a second degree black belt—got into a fight with a bunch of guys who supposedly were bikers. They were really just wannabes but they were dangerous. They had sticks and a couple of bottles. They had my guy on the wall and he was trying to fight them off. I came downstairs because I heard the commotion. I yelled out for everybody to stop. I guess because the music was so loud and they were so into it, they kept fighting. Anyway, it kind of pissed me off. So, I waded into these guys and they started falling. I don't know exactly how to describe it, but based on the way I move, they destroyed each other. I moved in such a way that everything that touched me, bounced off me and hit something else. It's like taking a basketball and spinning it on the floor and trying to drop quarters on it. The quarters are ejected because of what's happening with the ball. To some extent, that describes what I do.

**Called "King of the Katas"
in tournaments**

Chapter Ten
Meeting My Teacher

Another evening, as I was doing my rounds, checking on the various security stations, Louis Delgado came into the club looking for me. He tells me that Master Frank Ruiz is downstairs looking for me. I had no idea who that was, so Louis brings him up. At the time, he impressed me as a hard-looking dude. He wore a half black leather glove on his left hand and had a Van Dyke beard on his face. He sat there for a while and hung out. I had a nice talk with him, still not knowing who he was. He gets ready to leave and says to me in this gravely voice, "Hey Chaka, when I come back, these guys better not be in their gi tops." I immediately got pissed and thought to myself, "Who the f-k does this guy think he is?" I started to react stupidly, but said to myself, *hold on a minute, let me do my homework.* I said "Osu" (Okay). When I did my homework and found out who he was, it almost stopped my heart. Since I had been in the Marines and lived up in Harlem, I didn't know who he was but everyone else knew! Ruiz was a former Marine who had been awarded a Purple Heart, Bronze Star, Silver Star, and was the senior student of legendary Goju Supreme GM Peter Urban. He was a fifth degree black belt at the time. He used to say, "I'm the baddest mother-fkr around."

I've got a good story about him, to show you what kind of guy he was. While he was fixing a flat tire on his car on the Long Island Expressway, some kid (was) in a stolen car speeding at over 80 mph. Ruiz didn't see the car until it was almost on top of him but he jumped up and kicked it! They say that's the only thing that saved his life. He broke just about every bone in his body and they said he would never walk again. I went to see him in the hospital and all these Marine Colonels and Majors and Generals were coming to see him. That really impressed me and I'm hard to impress. However, three months later, he was in the dojo, training. I think that is because of his attitude as a Marine and that his body was in super shape. He loved to fight and used to fight us all the time. He used to beat the hell out of us, too (laughing out loud). But I think because his body was in such great shape, it saved his life. He was a very powerful man.

After I got out of the Marines, I had studied Chung Do Kwan—a (Tae Kwon Do) system—with Jung Ku Lee. I also studied with Thomas Bode, Peter Urban and Moses Powell but my main instructor has always been Frank Ruiz. He passed away in 1995 but he's still my teacher. There are several people who have claimed to be my teacher—or would like to claim me—but there's only one—Frank Ruiz.

There was no karate style called Nisei Goju when I met him. Nisei started the night he came to the Electric Circus and we all sat around him. It was automatic that we wanted to train with this guy. When we left work at the Circus that night, we went to the 7th Street dojo to train. It was Owen Watson's dojo at the time. Apparently young and full of vinegar, Ron Van Clief, upon meeting him, asked Master Ruiz if he wanted to spar. Big mistake! That was the night Van Clief ended up in the hospital.

For years, we never had a patch that represented our Nisei Goju System. We were a formidable group: Ron Van Clief, Earl Monroe, Owen Watson, Ronald Tagonashi, Louis Delgado, Herbie Thompson, Malachi Lee, Tom "La Puppet" Caroll, Rudy Winkfield, Joe Richardson, Skipper Ingham and myself. We would walk into a tournament—patch or no patch—and the place would clear out. Master Ruiz made a bunch of lunatics out of us. There were only a few schools doing anything at the time.

One day, I was walking downtown on Pell St. with Master Ruiz. I believe we were coming from Master Peter Urban's dojo. A big limousine had been coming up the street and stopped at the light. We had the right of way and started crossing the street. Just as we get in front of the limo, it jerks forward like it was going to hit us. Right away, we both got pissed off. We each ran around to either side of the car and snatched the doors open. *And, oh boy!* Sitting in the back seat were Mas Oyama and Tadashi Nakamura, and Shigeru Oyama was driving the car. I'm saying to myself, *What did I get myself into here?!* Scared the crap out of me. Then I look over to Master Ruiz and he and Mas Oyama are speaking (in Korean!) to each other, like they were old friends. They pulled the limo off to the side of the street and we all had a great time talking and laughing about the look on our faces when their car pulled up. It was a life changing experience, to know I was that close.

Master Ruiz really knew how to push our buttons. We were at S. Henry Cho's karate tournament in New York City. I had moved up to the finals in the kumite (fighting) competition. I had eliminated all of my competitors until there was no one to fight but one of our own Nisei black belts. It was Rudy Winkfield. Just before the fight, Rudy comes up to me and tells me that Master Ruiz told him to take it easy on me. He had a little smile on his face that enraged me. As a highly decorated combat Marine, Master Ruiz knew exactly how to get us motivated. As we fought, I felt the pressure of his attacks. Rudy was a skilled fighter, so I had to retreat a lot. The last time he attacked, I almost stepped out of the ring which would have forced me to lose. Instead, I whipped out a round house kick that slapped him in the face and knocked him flat on his ass. I won the match. I looked at him with pride, didn't say a word and walked off the mat.

I developed a kata (a choreographed sequence of movements), named it "Ja" and asked Master Ruiz if he would accept it as a green belt kata in Nisei. He said, "Chaka, if you enter the tournament with that kata and you win, I'll make it a black belt kata." So, I went to that tournament and I smoked it. I took first place and he made it a black belt kata. That kata is now included in my Zujitsu system.

One day, a group of us black belts, including Ron Van Clief, Owen Watson, Ron Tagonashi, Rudy Winkfield, Joe Richardson and Bob Chin, went up to Earl Monroe's dojo in the Bronx. We were all there to workout and spar with Master Ruiz. He took us on, one at a time. After he had fought a few of us, it was Bob Chin's turn. Before they started, Master Ruiz told Bob to watch his control. Even though Bob was also a trained Kung Fu practitioner, he had no sense of control. We had seen him working out in front of the mirror and actually break it with a kick. The very first punch he threw, hit Master Ruiz in the face. We were all sitting there watching. The look that came over Master Ruiz's face was deadly. Bob realized he had screwed up big time and started backing up swiftly towards the street door. I jumped up and yelled at Master Ruiz, reminding him that he was not in Korea and Bob was his student. He looked at me and broke out laughing. Meanwhile, Bob was outside peeking through the side of the door. By this time, we were all rolling on the floor with hysterical laughter. Bob came back and we had a great class.

Master Ruiz was well respected among his peers. One of his close friends was Peter Siringano, who had a dojo in Staten Island. Prior to his tournament, I was invited to go train with him at his dojo. I had a few reservations because I had seen what he did with his ukes (person who receives a technique). He was one rough customer. Many of his black belts (students) were often banged up by him but that did not stop me from going. I was excited and assumed he wouldn't hurt me, being one of Master Ruiz's black belts. I went to his dojo by myself, put on my gi and sat with the other students. First, we worked on several techniques. Eventually, we sat down again and this time, he called for an uke. I wanted to show his students that I wasn't afraid, so I volunteered. Fortunately, I was right. He was rough but he did not hurt me. That doesn't mean that I didn't feel it (laughing out loud)!

I had been invited to do a demonstration at Siringano's upcoming tournament. So, I practiced hard for several weeks. I had also made a Zulu costume that I intended to wear for my demo and had picked Zulu music for the performance. One of my senior black belts introduced me and made a speech about martial arts coming from Africa. Then, he started the music. I entered the crowded auditorium, walking down the aisle in costume. I got on stage and started my demo, displaying the use of the short Japanese sword, double knives, Bo, Sickle and a long chain. This was all before "musical forms" were included in tournaments. The crowd went crazy and I received three standing ovations. Grand Master Peter Urban jumped up on stage, grabbed my arm, shot it up into the air and yelled, "The New Grand Master" to thunderous applause. I was deeply honored. Later on, Siringano's wife was so impressed, that she invited me to his birthday party at their home in Staten Island.

I lived in several different places after moving down to The Village. I lived in a commune on Christopher Street, in a 6th floor walk-up apartment on East 10th Street with Ron Van Clief and at Skipper Ingham's dojo on 38th Street.

Skipper was quite a character. He would wear one of these huge Zorro-like hats, a shirt with huge puffy sleeves, high boots and a Samurai sword in his belt. During those days in the Sixties, everyone wore some crazy outfits, myself included. Skipper was actually an auxiliary police officer and had been a merchant marine for seventeen years. At some point, he moved back to Bermuda, his original home. He held annual tournaments and several of us went to support and compete. Flying was different then, with fewer regulations and those plane trips were one huge party. We all rented mopeds and were scooting around in our karate uniforms. Skipper threw some really good, well-organized tournaments with the help of his wife, Christine.

One of the guys I used to hang out with a lot, was Ron Tagonashi. He was an expert in breathing techniques and could bellow out a kiai (yell) that sounded like a wild beast. On one occasion, the two of us went down to St. Vincent's Hospital to do a demo. The room was full with doctors, nurses and patients. First, Tagonashi and I both did some self-defense techniques. Then, Tagonashi did a kata and got a great applause. So, I decided I was going to do Tensho kata, another breathing kata that is traditionally done without a gi top. I took off my gi top and began the kata, executing a middle block with a tension breath, tightening all my muscles. The room was absolutely silent when, all of a sudden, a woman in the audience loudly exclaimed, "OOOOH!" Well, I lost it. Everybody in the room fell out laughing. I laughed through the entire kata. What a wonderful memory.

We all hung out on St. Marks Place between 2nd and 3rd Avenues. It was our block and we made sure to protect it. Many of us were martial artists (and) some were just those who loved The Block. A lot of the gangs from Staten Island and Queens would come and start trouble and we would run them out. We weren't getting paid. We just loved the neighborhood, wanted to protect it, and had the skills to do it. Many "situations" occurred on that block.

On one occasion, my friend asked me to loan him three dollars. As I'm getting the money out of my pocket, this cop—a new guy on the block—runs over and demands to see ID. I said, "ID for what?" He says, "You guys are passing money and you might be passing drugs." The more he persisted, the more I resisted. He was getting more belligerent. Fortunately, another cop named Tony, who knew us all, started coming up the block. I said, "You see that officer there? You better go talk to him because you're about to get yourself in some trouble." By that time, a lot of the guys were there, crowding around this cop. After I explained to Tony what happened, he took this new cop aside and told him to *leave these guys alone. They don't do any drugs, or cause trouble. They protect the block and look after the people in the neighborhood.* That's exactly what we need, so leave them alone.

One day, I was sitting at the Dojo Restaurant. This was a popular place on St. Marks Place, owned by a Japanese friend of mine, Tony. I was wearing my flip flops, eating my meal, when one of my black belts, Jose, and another White guy come running by, chasing some Black guy. Now, both of them had knives in their hand and the Black guy is running for his life. He was so scared, that he ran right through the glass door where the Gypsies lived. I jumped up and to this day, I don't know how I got across the street without any shoes on. But *boom*, I was right in front of the Gypsy's place, just as Jose and his buddy got there. I yelled at Jose, "STOP!" Jose looked at me and stopped cold. His friend started to go again but I told him to stop, while he still had a chance. He looked at Jose and saw the look of fear on his face, then looked at me and stopped. He backed off, put the knife in his pocket and took off. Jose gave me his knife. I folded it and put it away. I found out later that the Black guy they were chasing, had offered them some drugs. They said they weren't interested but he was persistent. Jose's friend pulled out a knife and gave Jose one and the chase was on. I'm still surprised that the guy didn't kill himself, running right through that glass door.

Another time, in front of the Dojo Restaurant, some crazy woman came up behind Tony, the owner, and put him in a chokehold. Tony—being a judo black belt—responded automatically, by executing a shoulder throw, slamming her to the sidewalk. These three guys saw it happen and right away, they're ready to jump on Tony and beat his ass. Meanwhile, he's trying to explain to them what happened but has lost his English (and is) now in a panic. Since I had seen everything, I rushed up (again in my flip flops) and tried to explain it to them. These guys just didn't want to listen, so I asked if they were *looking for a fight, not to worry, they've found it*. I was ready to defend my friend. Then, one of the three guys who knew me said, "Zulu, I don't want no fight with you. No man, I don't want a fight with you." Now, these are big, tall guys and the other two are looking at him, wondering why their friend is in a panic to fight this little guy. He's looking scared to death because he knows how I can get—he's seen me like that before. They decided to back up, listen to what actually happened and leave it alone.

**Chaka Top Row, Third From the Left
Frank Ruiz, Far Left**

Chapter Eleven
My First Dojo

After a few years, I asked Master Ruiz if I could start teaching on my own. Someone had introduced me to the director of St. Marks Boys Home and I started a class there. I remember the first class, I was scared to death. I had taught in the dojo but that wasn't like my own school—with a whole bunch of people standing in front of me, waiting for me to teach them something. Some of the students, I already had from Master Ruiz's dojo, some of them were residents at the boys home and some came by word of mouth. Many people recognized me from the Electric Circus and as *one of the guys* who always protected the neighborhood. There were also less than a handful of dojos in the area at that time. Scared or not, I got over my fear by just going into Marine Corps mode. I believe in always leading the warm-ups. We would start running and I had this attitude that *if I'm in the front, no one else has any excuses.* I always led every workout. You can't lead from the rear. So, all of the running, the push-ups and sit-ups—all of it. Everything I made them do, I did along with them. I believe if you teach, teach by example, not with your mouth. I ended up having a great first class.

It was there that I developed a way to end class. I'd have everyone sit in a meditative position. I would take my obi (belt) off and whack each person on their back. Those people that flinched, I knew were not really meditating. Eventually, they all got to a point where they were able to blot it out and totally focus on their meditation. The other way we always end every class, is by hugging. The purpose of hugging is two-fold. First, to show affection for your dojo brothers, sisters, and teacher but it's also training. It's training because in life, most people are afraid to commit their bodies to each other, unless they are having sex. If you are a martial artist—especially if you are in any throwing systems—like judo or jujitsu—if you don't commit your body to your opponent, then you won't get the job done. You cannot throw from a distance and that means commitment.

We had many great times in that dojo. One of the unique situations occurred when a woman from Ecuador came to my school. She was well under five feet tall and had her ten-year-old daughter with her, who was the same height. Eventually, we found out the reason she started training was because her husband had been abusing her by burning her with cigarettes. When we found out, we wanted to hurt this guy but we didn't want to put her in any more difficulty. She had already separated from him and was now safe.

In any case, her daughter had a ponytail down to her calves. This got my creative juices running. I went out and got these sponge rubber balls at the dime store and tied them to her braids. I gave her exercises to do, swinging her head forward and back(ward), side-to-side, around in circles and figure-eights. This was in addition to her regular training with me. When I thought she had achieved what I gave her, I went down to Chinatown and bought these Chinese coins with the hole in the center. Then, I wove those into her braids. After a while I had her breaking boards with those braids. They eventually moved back to Ecuador and I hope they continued their training.

For many years, when I decided I had a little talent and that I could impart it to my students, I decided I wouldn't participate in any of the tournaments or demonstrations. *I'm just going to have my school and focus on my students. I'm not going to advertise in any newspapers* (this was before the Internet, of course). I believed if I *do all the right things* with my students, they will be the biggest, best advertisement. That's why I've always had a full dojo. If you focus on what you're supposed to, your students will bring their families and everyone else. I don't want to be famous—that's not my intent. I want to be able to fight—period. I don't think about anything else.

The Sign Outside the 2nd Avenue Dojo

Chapter Twelve

The 2nd Avenue Dojo

In 1973, Alan Levine, one of my black belts, took me up to a loft on Second Avenue, between 5th and 6th Streets. It had been a gay disco, and was painted all black. Alan said, "Look at this place. Do you think it could be a dojo?" I said, "Yes, it could be a dojo." He said, "Well, I just got it for you." The next day, some of my students and I began working on the place to make it a dojo. We cleaned and painted. It had a linoleum floor that had to be covered. So, I went to a carpet store to see what I could find.

When the owner came to measure the area, the students treated him with much respect and courtesy. It impressed him so much that he ended up covering the entire dojo floor and didn't charge me a penny! He would not let me pay for it. Then, my black belt Chester Catoose—who is a master carpenter—helped me build a loft bed in the back room. I moved in and lived there until the building was sold in 1981, when the new owners spiked the rent and forced me out.

I developed a big kids program in that dojo. I had sixty-two kids and many of them were children of the owners of the neighborhood restaurants and other businesses. It was great because since I lived in the dojo, they often brought me food from their restaurants or I would go there to eat. It was a real melting pot, including Gypsies, African Americans, Puerto Ricans, Chinese, Indian, Jewish and White Christians. We used to have sleepovers and go on picnics. I would take them to different dojos to meet other kids and train. I remember (a dojo) on Staten Island where a whole bunch of us went and had a great time working out with their students.

During those years I was teaching strictly Nisei Goju with my own touches. I guess I started Zujitsu subtly because I was dealing with many kids. I wanted to fight with them like I did with the adults but with a lot more concern for their safety. I instinctively knew that kids liked to roll and tumble on the floor—along with my training and rank in Judo—so I incorporated all (of) that into their training. Judo was my first love.

We had a lot of fun in that dojo. One of the ways I created to make money for the school was to have the "Barefoot Disco." This was held on Friday evenings. Everyone would take off their shoes before entering and line them up outside the door. Entry charge was three dollars. We had great music and would dance and party until 3am. It got really popular and went on for quite some time. That was the era of the discos! I was also working as a bouncer at several discos during that time—The Cheetah, The Church and Steve Paul's Scene, to name a few.

I remember when Steve Paul's Scene was having some problems with the gangsters. Steve Paul told me and Skipper to invite our guys to hang out there to help with security. One day, this woman was threatened by one of these guys (gangsters). She came running to me because she was scared to death. When I confronted him in front of the kitchen, I saw he had a pistol in his belt. I slapped the crap out of him and snatched the pistol. He's lucky I didn't shoot his ass. I jammed it in my belt and told him not to come here and threaten anyone, ever again. *Take it outside!* A few days later, I read in the paper that he committed suicide after killing his girlfriend and his dog.

Chapter Thirteen

Filming *The Warrior Within*

In 1976, a bunch of us went down to Puerto Rico to film *The Warrior Within*. This iconic film is one of the first-ever martial arts documentaries produced. Casting had been arranged by a colleague, Hui Cambrelen. It included several Asian practitioners besides our group. Later on, several other martial artists, like Chuck Norris, Bruce Lee, and Thomas LaPuppet Carroll were edited into the finished film. Our immediate group included myself, Ron Taganashi, Moses Powell, Lil John Davis, Alex Sternberg, and Florendo Visitacion. Also there was Dan Inosanto, Fumio Demura, Mike Stone, Pui Chan, Wai Hong, and Tom Ebihara.

(The film) represented the arts of Jeet Kune Do, Karate, Kung Fu, Jujitsu, Kendo, Tai Chi Chuan, and Oriental Weaponry. It received the Gold Medal Special Jury Award at the Las Americas Film Festival. We shot much of the film at El Morro Castle. When you listen to the opening scene, the voice you are hearing is mine. "You can curse my mother, my father, call me a faggot, call me a nigger, whatever you want to say, but the minute you put your hands on me, I'm going to hurt you, hurt you severely. That's a guarantee." That was the one thing they emphasized in the film. It's the way I thought then, and still the way I think now. You have to earn the right to hurt me.

I remember being on the castle wall during one scene. At the time, I was afraid of heights but no one knew. So we're standing on this sloping wall in the gun turrets and they don't tell us that they're bringing in a helicopter. All of a sudden it comes swooping in and the wind hits me. I went sliding down the edge of the turret toward the rocks. If I didn't have enough sense to jam my legs into the sides, I'd have fallen right down on the rocks. I was enraged and let everybody know.

A group of us including Master Ruiz, Moses Powell, Ron Tagonashi, Lil John Davis and I went out to eat at a local restaurant. We saw big signs all over, advertising our visit and upcoming demos. We all ordered tons of food and it was delicious. When the check came, and it's a big check, they handed it to Moses Powell. So he says, "What do you do if we can't pay this check?" The waiter responded, "We call the ambulance for you!" Well, we all broke out laughing, hysterically. Obviously, he did not know who we were. When he finally figured it out, he got white as a sheet. He couldn't believe what he had said to us. Moses Powell almost had a stroke, he was laughing so hard. We were all young then and we were full of piss and vinegar. It was hilarious and we all had a good laugh. Of course, we paid the check and gave him a huge tip. When he saw the tip, he couldn't believe it but Moses told him, "You were funny. You made us laugh. We had a good time and good food."

While we were (in Puerto Rico), every place I went to train, I was hanging out with Tagonashi. We would always try to pick a quiet location. One day, I realized Moses Powell was watching me. Finally, I got up the nerve and said, "Sensei, how come every time I turn around I see you watching me?" He said "Because I like what you do. I like how you move. I like to watch you move." I thanked him and went back to working out.

We had finished filming and we were all in this little hotel room. Powell was explaining some concepts and techniques to us. Every single time he would demonstrate a technique, one of the guys would come in with, "Well, we do it this way!" Just this one guy, everyone else was soaking up Powell's wisdom. I'm saying to myself, "This man is trying to give us some knowledge and you're acting like you're in competition with him." He should have just kept his mouth shut. I won't mention his name but later on, Powell invited me to train at his dojo—When Worlds Collide—in Brooklyn. He also specifically told me not to bring "that guy."

The first day I went to his dojo, I bowed in and Powell told me to go get dressed. I gi'd up and I had brought a white obi (belt) with me. I put it on and walked out onto the floor. Powell said, "What's that?" pointing at my white belt. I told him I knew nothing about Jujitsu, so I'm coming in as a beginner wearing a white belt. He told me to go back to the dressing room and put on my black belt or he'd kick my ass! So I did, and I had such a great time. I was sore as hell when I got out of there, but I had a great time.

I had the chance to workout with several of (Powell's) black belts and I learned so much. There was a key to what he was doing that I picked up and just brought it all together. *But my wrists!* My wrists were so damned sore and swollen and my hands, too. I was driving my Volkswagen with my forearms! The clincher for me that made me realize I had an instinct for what he was teaching, happened while I was working out with his black belts. GM Visitacion was there sitting on a stool, watching me and clapping his hands. I hadn't even realized he was there. Then he came up and showed me a few things. Yes, I've been lucky. I've been taught by some supreme martial artists. I've been very lucky.

Chapter Fourteen
When Walking Away Is Not An Option

The best kick in my mind, is the front kick. It's the most instinctive kick and if you perfect it, it will work every time. I'll give you a situation. I was coming out of a restaurant in Union Square with one of my female brown belts. As I'm getting ready to pay the check, the maître d' and the bartender are bum-rushing some guy out because he was causing a disturbance. They're yelling, "Get out of the way." So, we moved out of the way and let them take him out. I paid the check and we started walking down the stairs to go outside. Well, this guy is standing downstairs, looking up at us and starts yelling, "You niggers. You niggers." And I'm the only Black guy in the whole place. So, I'm walking down the stairs while this guy is screaming. I don't even remember my foot crashing into his chest. All I remember, is when he bounced off the car outside, my elbow went to meet him. He dropped like a stone. My hand clamped around his throat and I said to him, "Why are you using that word?" I was furious, but we just left.

Then, there was a restaurant downstairs from the dojo, owned by some nice people. One night they were having problems with a few guys who came in and started causing trouble. I had made friends with the owner of the place and told her if she had any issues, to just call upstairs. So, she called up and we came downstairs. As I recall, we were having a black belt class that evening and the dojo was full. We all put our shoes on and went downstairs. Within minutes of our arrival, all the issues got cleared up and those guys left.

Another time, I was at a Vietnamese restaurant about two blocks from the dojo with a female friend. We were eating and some Black guy came in. He immediately started carrying on, cursing and being obnoxious with the owners for no reason. I got up, went over and sat next to the guy. I picked up the fork and started fiddling around with it. Quietly, I said, "Look man, there's no need for all of that. I've got this woman over here and you're cursing and carrying on. These people ain't bothering you. Why are you doing all of that?" And I'm looking right in his eyes. He looked at me and figured out he was going to have a problem he might not be able to handle. I told him to calm himself down because if I come back *you better be prepared*. I walked away and sat back down at my table. He never said another word, took care of his business and left.

One night, I went to Chinatown and was having a meal at another Vietnamese restaurant. Paul Vizzio (a professional kickboxer) came in and we greeted each other with hugs and chatted, briefly. He was a great guy. He picked up his to-go order and left. When my dinner partner and I were finished, I asked for the check. The waiter said, "Check's been paid." Paul Vizzio had paid the check. Actually, the owner of the restaurant didn't want him to pay for the check because he wanted to comp the meal, himself. Turns out, he was also the owner of the Vietnamese restaurant where the Black guy came in and started to cause trouble. That was some instant good karma coming back to me.

Chapter Fifteen

Meeting Zosia Gorbaty

I met my wife, Zosia Gorbaty, at a Capricorn birthday party we were having at the dojo in December 1980. I was turning forty-two and a few other students had birthdays, as well. (Zosia) says I was very charming, kissing her hand old-fashioned style, when we were introduced. A few months later, she left the dojo—where she was a brown belt—to come and train at my school. By the end of 1981, we were a couple and have been together, ever since. That was also the year I lost the Second Avenue dojo because the building was sold. The new landlord forced us out by raising the rent to an unreasonable amount. For the next eighteen years, our dojo moved more than a dozen times. The good thing, is that every time, with every different space, our training had to change and adapt. The not so good thing, (was) losing some students along the way and the mundane tasks that go along with moving.

Chapter Sixteen
My Last Fight

For the first ten years we were together, we lived on the fourth floor walk-up of a brownstone building on East 88th Street. I had my last fight in that building a couple of years after we moved in. Zosia and I had been at a party and had an argument, so Zosia went home but I stayed. I drank far too much and was toasted by the time one of my black belts took me home. Determined to sleep on the couch, I started banging the furniture around and woke the downstairs neighbors. The guy came up, banged on our door and when I opened it, he was on the staircase, looking up. After some words, I was on the staircase looking down. It quickly escalated to throwing punches but I was too drunk to block. Next thing I see, is two arms coming from under my arms, blocking his punches. Zosia was behind me, blocking his punches! I was too drunk and as I grabbed the bannister, my thumb totally dislocated. The next couple of hours were spent at the hospital down the block, fixing my thumb.

We bumped into (the neighbor) and his girlfriend a few days later. I tried to apologize but he still acted like a jerk and only upset his girlfriend. Coincidentally, he moved out the following week. After all the violence and countless fist fights in my life, this was my last fight. That was over forty years ago. Now, at eighty-five years old, there would be no "fight." It would be a kill, only to defend myself or my wife.

I have developed a way to justify avoiding violent confrontations. I realized that when I have an altercation with someone, if there is no physical altercation and it's just verbal, I just end up beating myself up all day long saying to myself, "I

should have kicked his ass, I should have pummeled the guy, etc."
All day long, beating myself up because I didn't do what I think I
should have done. So I decided, in order to alleviate myself of all
that stress, as soon as any situation is resolved without violence, I
see the New York Times, in big block letters, "CHAKA ZULU
SAVED A LIFE TODAY." And I pat myself on the shoulder because
I didn't kill the fool. I also have a responsibility to my students
because I'm trying to teach them to be a certain way. If I'm going
to do the opposite, why would they want to train with me?

Chaka Showing Everyone How It's Done

It's your life; you don't need someone's permission to live the life you want. Be brave to live from your heart.

- Roy T. Bennett

The only way to do great work is to love what you do.

- Steve Jobs

Love the life you live. Live the life you love.

- Bob Marley

Part Two
Zosia Gorbaty

Chapter One

Early Years in Morningside Heights

I was born in Vienna, Austria in 1949, four years after the World War II (WWII) Holocaust that my Jewish parents had survived in Poland. For many years, I did not realize how intensely my childhood was affected by the horror my parents had experienced. As a youngster in the 1950s, I never heard the term "PTSD." It was not until I was well into adulthood that a friend—a Holocaust historian—made me aware of the residual effects the war had on my parents, that influenced my childhood.

When I was two years old, we moved to a six room apartment in Manhattan on 112 Street, between Broadway and Riverside Drive. This area is called Morningside Heights and is adjacent to the neighborhoods of both Harlem and Manhattan Valley. It was actually just over a mile from where my husband Chaka grew up but it might as well have been another country. We moved there because my father needed a place that allowed a piano where he could play and teach. That was his profession. My father was a magnificent pianist. He began playing at four years old and never stopped.

Our apartment was in a six-story, pre-war building with an elevator. At one time, it had been the residence of wealthy people. The small maid's room with a second toilet became my room. A little window faced the alley. It was tiny but it was all mine. My parents took the largest bedroom and rented out the other two bedrooms for much needed income. Since Columbia University was only a few blocks away, most of the renters were students. There were two large living rooms, separated by French doors that became my father's music studio. We had a large eat-in kitchen with an old fashioned dumbwaiter, that brought the trash down to the basement. The ceilings were at least nine feet high with beautiful, ornate crown moldings. We lived in that building until 1966. At some point, we moved to another larger apartment in the same building, where I got a real bedroom that faced the street. Across the street, on the corner was a huge billboard I could see from my window. It never changed. It read "The Wages of Sin is Death, but the Gift of God is Eternal Life." As a Jewish child I had no idea of its meaning or that it was a quote from the Christian Bible: Romans 6:23. This quote is still such a vivid memory. Ironically—directly across from my window—there was a residence hotel where occasional "interesting" views were possible.

Many folks in our few-block-radius neighborhood were also immigrants from various European countries. My mother's two best friends were also Holocaust survivors, from Romania and Hungary. They both, each had little girls my age who became my best friends—Pearline and Jacqueline. Pearline lived a block away and Jacqueline lived in an apartment across the hall from me. Our early years were spent playing in the sandbox down the block in Riverside Park. I remember being jealous of Jacqueline because although her mother was Jewish, her father was Greek Orthodox. So, she celebrated both holidays to take off from school.

My father did his best to engage me in physical activities. He taught me how to ride a bicycle and how to ice skate. We would go to the Wollman Rink in Central Park. My young summers were spent at Camp Music Land, where he was a teacher and my mother would commute to the city, daily to work. Every summer, the camp would have a production of various musicals. I was only five when I was one of the children in *The King and I*. When I was eleven, we rented a cottage on Round Lake in Monroe, New York. That's where he taught me how to fish. We would catch little sunfish and toss them back.

Our Manhattan neighborhood was filled with many small mom-and-pop stores on Broadway. On the corner, was "The Cleaners", Asian operated, where we brought my father's shirts and suits and my mother's dresses. Next to it, was Anita's Dress Shop. This is where my mother bought all her clothes for work. My mother started working when I began kindergarten at age five. Unfortunately, her teaching credentials from Poland were not recognized here. So, she got a part time job as a personal assistant to a wealthy woman. Then she had a series of office jobs with The American Thread Company, JVC Electronics and finally became Director of Accounts Receivable for the CBS subsidiary publishing company of Holt, Rhinehart and Winston. She retired from that position at seventy-five years of age, traveling by subway from Queens to Manhattan, every day. Although she could have retired sooner, she really enjoyed her job and staying busy.

My favorite store was the chocolate shop, a couple of blocks away on Broadway. It was filled with the finest, delicious, homemade chocolates. My mother used to take me there every so often as a special treat. I always got the same truffles and turtles. The truffles had two layers of melt-in-your mouth chocolate. The turtles, either milk chocolate or dark chocolate, had sweet caramel and nuts. They either had almonds or pecans and were shaped like little turtles. They are still some of my most favorite chocolates.

The local pharmacy was on the corner of 110th Street and Broadway, called Rexall. It had a diner-type counter that served food. When I was old enough, my mom would give me lunch money once a week to eat there. I felt like such a grown-up, eating at the counter. My meal was always a cheeseburger, fries and a chocolate malted. I can't remember how much it cost back then, but I do remember going to the pizza shop after school with my friends. For a quarter, we got a slice and a coke.

The neighborhood where we shopped did not go east of Broadway. There, it changed from primarily European immigrants to Manhattan Valley where mostly Puerto Rican and Dominican immigrants lived. My grade school, P.S. 165, on 109th Street between Broadway and Amsterdam was ninety percent Latino. "Interesting" how they separated the few White and Asian students into a different class, all the way from first to sixth grade. Only two Puerto Rican girls were in my class: Iris and Diana. Sadly, my parents had been led to believe they were a "bad influence" because of their race and I was not allowed to befriend them. I could not understand why, however, so they became my secret friends.

I remember going over to Diana's home. She lived in a walk-up building off Columbus Avenue. It was a railroad apartment with the kitchen and living room in the front and bedrooms in the back. The smells from the kitchen were delicious and unfamiliar. To this day, Puerto Rican and Dominican food are some of my favorites. Stewed chicken, plantains (either maduro sweet or tostones garlicky), rice and beans.

I also remember cutting school to go to what they called a "set" or a party. It was at someone's house, whose parents were at work. Everyone there was playing hooky for the afternoon. I was in J.H.S. 54 by then. It was located in Manhattan Alley on Columbus Avenue and 108th Street. This was the Latino enclave of the many nationalities that settled in Manhattan. The music was mostly slow R&B and the dancing was really just grinding. We were all at the precipice of our adolescence with raging hormones and curiosity. Of course, I never told my parents about these escapades.

**Left:
Jan Gorbaty**

**Right:
Judith Gorbaty**

Chapter Two
Holocaust Legacy

My parents had quite a robust social life. As more Polish Jews arrived in New York City after the war, many were musicians or classical music lovers. After finding each other, a network was formed. They loved to get together to eat, drink, chat and sing Polish folk songs. The calendar on our kitchen wall was filled with invites for the Saturday evening gatherings. They all rotated and gatherings at our house, were two or three times a year.

The New Years Eve party at our house became a regular affair. I remember sneaking some spiked punch once and paying for it the next day. Most of the attendees had lost family during the invasion of Poland by the Nazis and a few had tattooed numbers, given to those prisoners from Auschwitz. According to Wikipedia, "The official name, Auschwitz Birkenau German Nazi Concentration and Extermination Camp (1940-45)...The Polish government has preserved the site as a research center and in memory of the 1.1 million people who died there, including 960,000 Jews, during World War II and the Holocaust." Everyone would gather around the piano to sing, as the folk songs were played. This is the part that I knew—not the horrors of war that they had all experienced. My mother continued to host these New Years Eve parties until she retired from working and slowed down at seventy-five years or so.

Growing up, I had no idea of the residual effects of WWII on my parents. My mother kept her pain from me. I don't know how she managed to move on with such amazing strength and fortitude, after losing so many—over twenty-seven members—of her family. Mother, father, two sisters, brother-in-law, niece and countless cousins. Her absolute bravery—to work for the Germans in their offices, speaking fluent German—to survive, living under an alias name and identity. She will always be my hero. On the other hand, my father was not one to hold in his emotions. It was not uncommon for him to yell, often lashing out at my mother. Whenever I asked her why she would not object, her answer was, "He doesn't mean it. He's just nervous. In one ear, out the other." I could never understand what that meant at the time but I realize now it was his PTSD from WWII. I remember he would seem to explode for the most unnecessary reasons. After he yelled, he would go to his piano and play. My father was an amazing pianist and a very charismatic man. It is said that women *often marry men that have similar traits to their fathers*. This definitely rings true for me, marrying a charismatic man with exceptional creative abilities, who also suffers from PTSD.

My father was born in 1915 Woloczyska, Russia, close to the Polish border. He had an older sister and brother. The family was considered wealthy and there was a nanny for my young father. Unfortunately, because they were of the Jewish faith, the family was forced out of Russia during the Pogroms of 1917. Most of their possessions were confiscated by the Bolsheviks and they had to begin again in a new country. They settled in Lwow, Poland. This is where my father's amazing talent as a pianist began to be apparent at the age of four years old. Sadly, just a few years later, his father died, unexpectedly. I recently found a piece of a Polish newspaper article about his untimely death in my treasured archives, passed down to me. The article translates to "he dropped dead in the street."

My grandmother, Malka, was left to raise her three children alone, in pre-war Poland. Young Malka was a strong and stately-looking woman from the photos I have seen. She managed to survive and provide for her family. When I finally met her (as a little girl), we were never able to have a conversation because she never learned to speak English. She only spoke Polish, Russian and Yiddish—all fluently. I remember visiting her in Brighton Beach, Brooklyn, often known as Little Russia. We would always stop at the famous Mrs. Stahl's knish store on the way. Potato and kasha knishes were my favorite. What a treat. Perfectly seasoned mashed potato or kasha surrounded by a thin, crispy crust. Cut it in half, hold it like a sandwich and dip it into mustard with every bite. When we arrived at her house, I would kiss her hello, take my knish and go watch the little black and white TV in the other room. She passed away when I was twelve and I am so sorry I never got to hear any stories about her life. I miss the kind of special relationship that I see others have with their grandparents. She was the only grandparent I would ever meet.

Malka's other children—Jack and Beba—were about twelve years older than my father. Life in pre-war 1930's Poland was tentative at best for Jews. Many thousands of German Jews were leaving for other countries and soon, Jews in Poland were doing the same. By this time, my father's career as a budding concert pianist was in full bloom. He had become the youngest faculty member at the prestigious Warsaw Conservatory of Music. He had also recently met his future wife, my mother. He could not leave Poland now but Malka and her other adult children, fearing for the future, would not stay.

On April 6, 1939, Malka received her U.S. immigration visa. Together, the three boarded the MS Batory and arrived in New York on May 2, 1939, leaving Jan in Poland. German forces invaded Poland just a few months later in the early hours of

Friday, September 1, 1939. I have very few photos of my young father, since all was lost during the war, except for the photos taken to the U.S. by Malka.

My mother, Judith, was born in 1913 Kuty, Poland. She was the middle child of three sisters. Her mother was a wonderful baker and her father worked for the railroad. They kept a Kosher home with separate plates for meat and dairy. Education was important and my mother achieved a Masters Degree in Latin and Greek from the university in Lwow, where she met my father. She actually spoke several other languages, as well, including Polish, Russian, Yiddish, German and eventually English. Her linguistic skills would come in very useful in the future. Her older sister was married and had a little girl. She had a comfortable and happy childhood.

Before WWII, she worked as a teacher of Latin and Greek in a high school in Sopot, Poland. She never spoke much about her family and I never knew she had any sisters, until I was about nine years old. I knew both her parents were killed in the Holocaust but she never spoke of her sisters, until then. My mother kept her grief to herself. I can't imagine the unbearable pain she kept inside. I will never forget that I was sitting in the kitchen, playing with my plastic silver colored cutlery set, when she came to me and said she needed to tell me something. She said, "I had two sisters, one older, one younger. My older sister was married and had a little girl. They were all killed by Hitler." I asked her why she had waited so long to tell me. I know now, like most mothers, she wanted to save me from the sadness and grief she felt.

1940 Poland was in turmoil but my parents were young, in love and had to be together. So, on July 6, 1940, they got married. They never spoke about a wedding or ceremony. I'm sure there was no big celebration, as life in Warsaw was becoming more and more difficult for Jews. Many deportations were already taking place. Without cell phones or the Internet, Hitler was able to gain power by deception and lies. Communication was often impossible. Even when people were being sent to gas chambers, they were told they were going to the showers and would receive fresh clothing and food afterwards. Of course these were all lies but they did not know it. Entire villages of Jews were herded together and forced to walk miles and miles. Supposedly, they were going to Labor Camps to work for the Nazis but often, once they arrived, only the strong men and a few women would be saved to work for them. Most of the women, children, and elders were "disposed of" by gas or bullets and thrown into mass graves. Eventually, the graves were so overfilled that they had the "laborers" dig them up to be burned in huge bonfires. This way, the Nazis could also hide their mass killings.

During one such deportation, my parents were in a huge crowd of Jews being herded through the city, supposedly on their way to a Labor Camp. There were thousands of people walking day and night and in the commotion of it all, my parents got separated. I cannot imagine the panic they must have felt. Amazingly, they had a special whistle that was a short phrase of six notes from one of my father's piano pieces. I can hear it now in my head and will never forget it. My father began whistling this phrase until my mother heard it and they reunited. During the next night of walking through a town with the crowd, they made their escape into a building and hid until they were safe.

Although they rarely spoke about "the War," I do remember one other poignant story. They were living in Warsaw where many people lost their homes and possessions. It was common for many people to share one house, living in one room with a shared bathroom and kitchen. On one occasion, the Gestapo was going from house to house, looking for Jews. They were rounding them up to be deported to "Labor Camps." If someone did not move fast enough or tried to hide and was caught, they were gunned down on the spot. My parents lived in one of these rooms and heard the commotion. They heard the gunshots. My mother began to gather her belongings and was ready to go. My father told her to put down her things, go sit in the corner where the light was dim and smoke a cigarette. She did as was told, sitting in the dark where her more "Jewish" features could not be clearly seen. Fortunately, my father's blue eyes and fair hair gave him the ability to easily pass for a member of the Aryan race. Soon came a strong knock at the door. My father opened the door and faced the gun-toting Gestapo Nazi. With a look of defiance, my father said, "What do you want here?" The Nazi looked at him, then at my mother sitting in the corner smoking a cigarette and then back at my father and said, "Sorry to bother you. We are looking for Jews," and he left. That was my father—strong, passionate, defiant, creative, brave and headstrong. And it probably saved their lives.

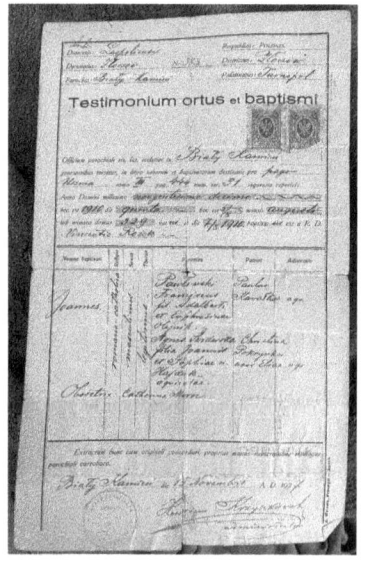

False Birth Certificates

Giving My Parents New Identities

New German Identification Cards "Kennkarte"

Soon after this incident, my parents were able to secure false birth certificates, that identified them as Polish Catholics. My father's new name became Jan Pawlowski and my mother became Maria Worliczek. These birth certificates then allowed them to secure a gray-green "Kennkarte"—the identification card color issued to Poles (non-Jews). These were obligatory ID cards, ordered in 1939 under the decree of Governor Hans Frank to be issued to all non-German citizens, who were at least sixteen years old. The card color for Jews and Gypsies was yellow—for Russians, Ukrainians, Belarusians, Georgians and Highlanders, was blue. These cards also indicated residence, birth information, profession and fingerprints. Maria was identified as a Roman Catholic policewoman and Jan as a Roman Catholic musician. Securing these new identities gave them some relief but now, in the eyes of the government, they were not married. This added to their fears of being caught but they persevered.

My mother's extraordinary linguistic abilities became more valuable than ever. She was able to secure a job, working in an office for the Germans. How stressful it must have been and what bravery and stamina was needed to maintain her false identity.

While working for them, she was also given extra potatoes and bottles of Vodka, which she exchanged for food. Everything of any value, including her wedding ring, had already been sold for food. My father continued working as a music teacher and chorus conductor, sometimes being required to play for the Germans. It is said, the Nazis enjoyed music while they sent Jews to the gas chambers because it drowned out the cries of the people. This is how my parents lived and survived until the Liberation in May 1945.

After the Liberation, everyone who survived, registered and began searching for their loved ones. Not one family member from either side of the family who was living in Poland when the war began, survived. My parents told me they stopped counting at twenty-seven family members, just on my mother's side. They were alone but they were together in war-torn Warsaw. With hope in their hearts, they soon left their homeland for Vienna, Austria. They registered with the International Refugee Organization and were issued Displaced Persons or Refugee Identity Cards. They were finally able to take back their real names.

Their ultimate goal was to immigrate to the United States but that was not such an easy task. In order to come to the U.S., you had to have family members there and prove they would support you, so you would not become a financial burden to the government. There were countless letters from my father's sister and brother and my mother's two uncles. They were the only family members left, besides my father's mother because they left Poland before Hitler invaded. No matter, it took many letters and applications and wasn't until five years later, that they saw U.S. soil. During that time, my father resumed his music career and my mother resumed teaching, until she got pregnant.

On April 1, 1949, April fools Day, I was born in Vienna, Austria. I was told my mother was in the hospital for a couple of days before the birth. Apparently my father could not be reached when my mother finally delivered me, so the hospital left a message at their residence, saying I was born. When my father arrived home, it took some time to convince him. He would not believe it, saying they were *just playing an April fool's joke* on him. Eventually, he took a chance and went to the hospital. Obviously it was true. They said I had so much hair when I was born, that the nurses put it in a little ponytail. People still remark at what a great head of hair I have, all thanks to my good genes.

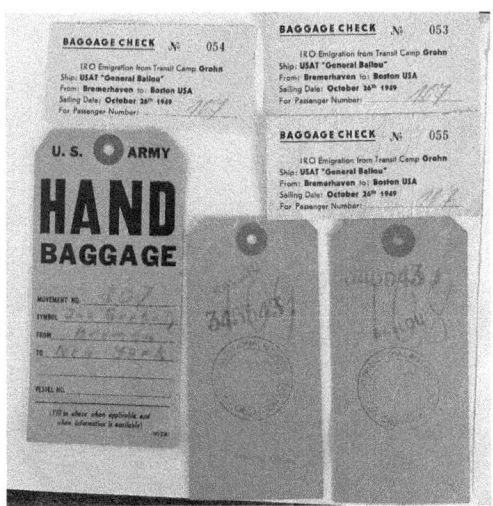 A few months after I was born, they received the good news that we were granted permission to emigrate to the U.S. It had been a long wait. We were first transferred to Camp Grohn in Bremerhaven, Germany. This was the largest displaced persons camp after the war, housing as many as five-thousand persons, prior to emigrating to the U.S. or elsewhere. Finally, on October 26, 1949, we sailed away on board the General C. C. Ballou, bound for Boston. Me in a basket, my parents and whatever worldly goods could fit in three suitcases with baggage check numbers 053, 054, 055. This ship—with accommodations for up to three-thousand—made sixteen voyages, between Germany and the U.S., with displaced persons from 1949 to March, 1950, when it was returned to the U.S. Navy. The Ballou

was definitely not a fancy cruise ship. My parents told me the seas were very rough on that voyage. Everyone on board ship got seasick, except me. When we finally arrived at Boston Harbor, November 5th, an older gentleman at the pier came over, placed a dollar bill in my basket and told my mother it was for good luck in the new country. From Boston, we boarded a train bound for New York City, where family was waiting for us.

My father's older brother had done well for himself. He was married and had a young son. He had bought a building in Maspeth, Queens, where he operated a grocery store and had a small two-room apartment above. That apartment became our home for the next couple of years. This was also where my love affair with music began. Fortunately, my father was able to secure a small upright piano to continue his practice and career. Since the place was very small, my crib was situated next to the piano. Apparently, I was told that I would sleep through most of his practice time, which was about six hours a day. Whenever I would wake up, I would lift up my head, look around and go back to sleep. Listening to my father playing the piano is what I miss most, now that he is gone. We lived in that two-room apartment until we moved to Manhattan.

Chapter Three

The Piano

When I turned five years old, my father became my piano teacher. He was a magnificent, accomplished pianist. My parents' friends used to ask me, "Will you be following in your father's footsteps? Will you become a great pianist?" That pressure on a child just made me upset. Having him as my piano teacher really strained our relationship. It did not last long because even at that age, I was defiant. Our arguments resulted with him sending me to learn from one of his colleagues. This was at the Third Street Settlement Music School, located in the East Village of Manhattan. It was established in 1894 and is still operating.

Every Saturday morning, my mother and I would get on the Number One subway at Broadway and 110th Street, then change to the F train at 42nd Street to finally arrive at our stop on Houston Street. We would spend a few hours at the school. Not only did I have piano class but also music theory, sight singing and composition. In addition, I was required to perform in their recitals. These were held every few months. I remember sitting backstage, waiting for my turn to play, butterflies in my tummy, just wanting it to be over. I still have many of the paper programs listing my name and pieces I played.

Although I didn't really want to perform, I'm so grateful now that I had the experience. It also prepared me to audition for the prestigious High School of Music & Art. After music school, my mother and I would often walk up 1st Avenue to the Polish store to get kielbasa and pierogi to bring home. I was required to practice piano for an hour every day after school. It wasn't my choice but my parents said, "Some day you will appreciate this." At the time, I resented my father for making me practice daily. However, now I am so appreciative of being able to play!

I did not have a strong religious upbringing. My father declared he was an atheist. He had lost his belief after experiencing the horrors of WWII. My mother, who had been brought up in a Kosher home, still maintained her Jewish faith. Although our kitchen was not Kosher, my mother made sure our Chanukah candles were lit, we attended a Passover Seder, she fasted on Yom Kippur and that she lit candles (called Yahrzeit candles) for the family who had passed. I was sent to Hebrew school, once a week for a couple of years. I believe it was during that time, I decided I would not wear a Jewish Star charm around my neck, hoping my blond hair, blue eyes and straight nose would allow me to pass for a "Gentile" (non-Jew), so I could avoid persecution. This feeling of wanting to hide my Jewish faith has followed me all my life. I believe it is part of my genetic trauma.

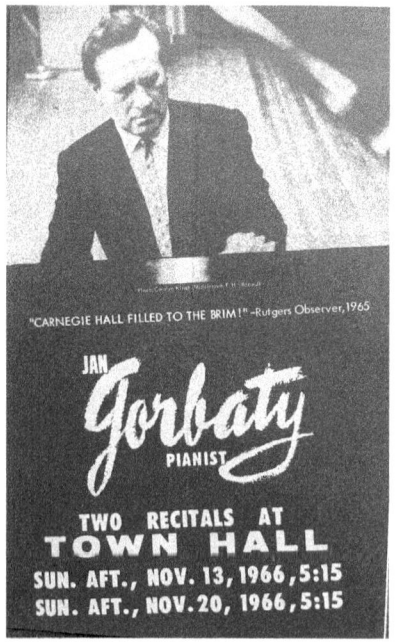

My Daily Piano Practice Begins

Left: Jan Gorbaty, Pianist

Chapter Four
High School of Music and Art

By 1962, I was ready to go to high school. I was only thirteen, but had skipped over third grade with the rest of my mostly White class in P.S. 165. Then, I was placed in the "SP" two-year instead of three-year program, in junior high school. These were all decisions based on race and culture, although I did not know it at the time.

During most of my younger years, from the age of five, music was a big part of my life. Although my father's career, as a young protege pianist, was interrupted by the war, he was able to resume it in New York. His primary studio was in our home but he was also on the faculty of the Chatham Square Music School, the New York College of Music, New York University and Rutgers University. He met a wealthy man, who became his patron. He would go downtown to the Plaza Hotel to have lunch with him and discuss his career.

My father gave concerts at Town Hall, Carnegie Hall and Lincoln Center, as well as many small venues. I attended all his main concerts with my mother. After the concerts, there were always long lines of people who wanted to congratulate him and take photos. It was like he was a rock star. He loved to keep his hair long in an artistic way because it was dynamic as he played. When I was older, I was the only one allowed to trim his hair. Chopin was his favorite composer and he became president of the New York Chapter of the International Chopin Foundation. He organized many concerts at the Polish Consulate, bringing in other performers, as well. He gave his last performance there in May, 1999 before he passed.

Fortunately, my mother was very secure about their marriage. I never saw any jealousy or discomfort from her. On the contrary, my mother was the one keeping it all together. She was in control of all the practical aspects of their life, allowing my father the freedom to focus on his creative musical life. My father was a devoted pianist, practicing for many hours every day. For many years, until I turned eighteen and moved out, I was used to hearing him practice. I sure do miss listening to him play but fortunately do have his one CD to still appreciate.

Achieving entry into the High School of Music & Art (M&A) opened up a new world. I now had to take a bus to get to school and then walk up a big hill. M&A was up in Harlem, next door to the City College of New York. I passed their entry exam on piano performance but was required to now take an orchestral instrument, as well. I really was not interested in playing an orchestral instrument. What I really wanted to do was to learn how to play jazz piano. That was my dream but I had no choice and was assigned the oboe.

The oboe is a wind instrument that sits near the clarinets in the orchestra. It uses a double reed, unlike the clarinet's single reed and is quite a challenge. Not only do you need breath control but you must develop your embouchure (the particular way to apply your mouth to the mouthpiece). At that time, I had no idea this introduction to breath control and diaphragmatic breathing would be a lifelong focus. I played the oboe in the school orchestra and sitting in the seat next to me, also playing an oboe, was Michael Kamen. Michael became an excellent composer and went on to create the musical scores for many well known movies, like *Lethal Weapon*, *Die Hard*, and *License to Kill*. We bumped into each other again in 1973 at The Lake nightclub in Woodstock, NY, where I was working at the time. It was great to see him and reminisce. Unfortunately, he passed away in 2003 at only fifty-five years old—a tragic young talent, lost too soon.

Another one of my friends at M&A was Laura Nigro. Laura and a few of us girls would meet in the school bathroom to sing harmonies. Motown singing groups were very popular at the time and the acoustics in the bathroom were wonderful. It was great fun. Laura later changed her last name to Nyro and went on to write several hit songs and record a few albums. She is best known for "Wedding Bell Blues" and "Stone Soul Picnic." Sadly, we lost her too soon, as well—from ovarian cancer—in 1997 at only forty-nine years old.

As a high school student, I became aware of the world around me. "By the 1960's, decades of racial, economic, and political forces, which generated inner city poverty, resulted in race riots within minority areas in cities across the U.S." —*Wikipedia*

On August 28, 1963, two-hundred fifty thousand people peacefully marched on Washington, D.C., demanding voting rights and equal opportunity for African Americans and to appeal for an end to racial segregation and discrimination. Martin Luther King gave his famous *I Have a Dream* speech. "I have a dream that my four little children will one day live in a nation where they will not be judged by the color of their skin but by the content of their character."

On November 22, 1963, at 2:30pm EST in Dallas Texas, President John F. Kennedy was assassinated. This was an event that was so egregious that the entire nation—no—the entire world was in mourning. I remember the moment I heard the news. I was on the bus that Friday afternoon, returning home from Music &

Art H.S. The news traveled like wildfire. Everyone was in disbelief. People were openly crying in the bus and in the street. JFK was a beacon of light for so many people, for so many young people, for the entire nation. Little did we know that was just the beginning of the 1960's assassinations.

The following year on July 2, 1964, President Lyndon Johnson signed the Civil Rights Act into law. It prohibited discrimination in public places, provided for the integration of schools and other public facilities, and made employment discrimination illegal. It prohibited discrimination on the basis of race, color, religion, sex, or national origin. However, although the law changed, many opinions would not, resulting in much violence. "Between 1964-71 there were more than 750 race riots, killing 228 people and injuring 12,741 others. After more than 15,000 separate incidents of arson, many Black urban neighborhoods were in ruins." —NY Times, December 30, 2004

On February 21, 1965 Malcolm X was assassinated, gunned down on stage at the Audubon Ballroom in NYC. Unlike MLK and others, he advocated the liberation of African Americans "by any means necessary." He was admired by his community but became too powerful for some.

Chapter Five
My First Lesson in Self-defense

My first introduction to self-defense awareness occurred one afternoon when I was about fourteen. I did not have any experience with violence or assault before that afternoon. I had gone out to the local store to buy a book. Our building had an outside entry door, then a few steps up to an inside entry door. Occasionally, the inside door would be locked at night but during the daytime neither door was ever locked. Inside were ground floor apartments on either side and a large lobby. At the end on the left was the stairway and mailboxes. On the right was the elevator. It had the usual door to pull open and then the sliding inside door that shut, so it could operate.

As I was waiting for the elevator to come, a White man walked into the lobby. He had no outstanding features or unusual attire. When the elevator arrived, I got in, pressed my floor and stood in a corner with my head in my new book. The man came in after me, pressed a floor button and took stance in the opposite corner. The outside door slammed shut. Then, as the sliding door began to close, something told me to look up from my book. As I did, I saw he had unzipped his fly and his penis was out of his pants.

I immediately responded by going for the door. Fortunately, it had not slid closed yet and I was able to push the outer door open. With my adrenalin pumping, I ran six blocks to my friend Irene's house on 106th Street. Once there, I called my parents to let them know what happened. My mother, father and dog Skippy came to get me and walk me home.

I was lucky that day and the incident taught me my first self-defense lesson. I never got into an elevator with a stranger ever again. I never even waited in my lobby with a stranger again. If anyone came into the lobby while I was waiting for the elevator, I would declare, "oh, I forgot to get the milk," and I would walk outside until I felt it was safe. I also made it a habit to check the reflective mirror, that showed if anyone was hiding under the staircase.

Young Zosia With Skippy

Chapter Six

Growing Up is Hard to do

After High School, I attended Hunter College in the Bronx, now known as Lehman College. It was 1966, I was seventeen and in my second year of college. I was living with my parents in their Forest Hills, Queens townhouse where we had moved the previous year. Then, I got pregnant. I was in a panic. What should I do? I had my whole life ahead of me. Having a baby now was not in my plans. What would my parents say? Roe vs. Wade had not yet happened. Abortions were illegal, and horror stories of back room abortions were commonplace.

After many inquiries, I was directed to a gynecologist who performed illegal abortions in his office. He was located in an upscale Manhattan neighborhood, 79th Street by Park Avenue. The fee would be eight-hundred dollars, cash. That was a lot of money for me then and I was only able to raise seven-hundred dollars, with the help of my boyfriend. Thankfully, he accepted that amount. I was to arrive at his office after his last patient.

I remember sitting in the small waiting room of his brownstone. I had a hard time controlling my nerves. Finally, it was time. I walked upstairs to his office. We were the only two people there. He gave me an injection of something to make me woozy but keep me awake. I was only about six weeks pregnant so it wouldn't take too long. I remember lying there, my feet in the stirrups, feeling him scraping out my insides. I really wasn't aware of the time. When it was over, I got dressed. He told me to expect some bleeding but to go to the hospital, if I hemorrhage. I was still feeling the effects of the drug but made my way down the stairs.

My boyfriend picked me up and drove me to the home of friends Jay and Peter, where everyone was watching *Star Trek*. *Star Trek* was a new show on TV and had gained popularity quickly. A group of us would gather at their apartment to watch it. I laid down on the couch and fell asleep. Fortunately, I recovered with no adverse effects.

Today, it seems like a bad dream. I was one of the lucky women who survived without complications. Unfortunately, many women who did not have the money or connections had abortions in less than acceptable medical conditions and did not survive. I am so upset about the political climate now that has made abortion illegal again in many states. Making it illegal again will only push women into unsanitary and unsafe abortions conditions. These laws will not stop them.

Meanwhile, more violence was erupting in the streets. On April 4, 1968, Reverend Martin Luther King Jr. was assassinated at the Lorraine Motel in Memphis, Tennessee.

A few months later on June 5, 1968, Robert F. Kennedy was assassinated. He was shot at the Ambassador Hotel in Los Angeles, California and pronounced dead, the following day. He was a U.S. Senator at the time and the leading candidate in the 1968 Democratic presidential primaries.

Chapter Seven
My Hippie Life

The '60s also marked the "Hippie Movement." This is where "people, mainly younger folks, were trying to break away from society's values that were being placed on them. They did this by protesting what they saw wrong with the world, including the Vietnam War." — *www.quora.com*

Often, college students are up in front of politics and the latest movements. I was one of them. I embraced the anti-establishment movement and was determined to live life my way. "Make Love, Not War," was our motto. "Flower Power" not weapons. "Tune In, Drop Out." Communal living, free love, psychedelics, equal rights for everyone, anti-war protests, brown rice and tofu, yoga, Bob Dylan, Joan Baez and Joni Mitchell. It was a time of protest and social justice.

Then, in 1966, I was introduced to a man—a guru—who would have an indelible impact on my life.

"Swami Satchidananda was one of the first yoga masters to bring the classical yoga tradition to the West after he was invited to America in 1966 by pop artist icon Peter Max." —*integralyoga.org*

"...'I didn't know what a swami was,' Max said. But he was instantly mesmerized by the Indian man with golden eyes. 'I just told him, Swami, America needs you desperately to come there. All the hippies were running around, experimenting, trying to become sort of enlightened.'

Under a visa identifying him as 'Minister of Divine Words', the Swami came for a two-day visit, but wound up staying for the rest of his life. He became a popular yoga teacher in New York City.

Within a year, his supporters had bought him a $1-million center on Manhattan's Upper West side." --*LATimes.com*

That is where I met him at his apartment on West End Avenue. I went there with a group of my friends from college and we all became hooked. I was immediately drawn to yoga philosophy and the physical practice. We all hoped yoga would be a path to the enlightenment we sought. The breathing exercises were already familiar to me from my oboe practice but the physical and meditation practices were new and challenging. I loved the idea of connecting my mind, body and soul. The new experience of meditation helped clear my mind and helped me relax. I liked the idea of no competition, except with oneself. I had no idea I would become a yoga teacher to college students, many years later.

College, however, was not a priority. In December 1967, I dropped out of school, got married to my boyfriend since "living together" was not acceptable then and we drove to San Francisco. Our time there—less than a year—was filled with music, psychedelic drugs and yoga. I was at The Fillmore Auditorium or Avalon Ballroom every weekend, dancing to Jimi Hendrix, Janis Joplin, Country Joe & the Fish, Grateful Dead, Santana, Creedence Clearwater Revival and Quicksilver Messenger Service. I would take a bus and go alone. I always wore my long, flowing dress, made of shiny silver material. I loved the music, and I loved to dance. My then husband was always off somewhere else.

During the week, I worked at a downtown company that sold advertising airtime on TV. My husband registered to be a substitute teacher but I later discovered he would turn off the phone ringer every morning, so as not to receive any calls into work. When I finally came to my senses—less than a year later—we returned to New York and got divorced. It was a "quickie divorce" that took place in Juarez, Mexico over a weekend. I flew down there alone and stayed at a hotel where it appeared that almost everyone there was also getting a divorce. All the men were flirting with the women and all the women wanted nothing to do with the men. On Monday morning, a bus came to pick up everyone and bring us to the town hall. One by one, our names were called. Each person went up to the front and signed the necessary divorce papers. The same bus then took us all to the airport for our flights home.

It was time for me to get back to school. I returned to Hunter College and got my Bachelor's degree in February 1971, majoring in English Literature with a minor in Theatre. Now I was ready to see the world. My friend Carol and I made plans to go to Europe but she backed out at the last minute. I decided to go by myself, anyway. Nothing was going to hold me back.

My Hippie Life

Chapter Eight

Backpacking through Europe

My first stop would be London. The plane ticket was two-hundred dollars. As was common at that time, I carried most of my money in traveler's checks. My friend Janet had already moved to London, so I knew I could stay there for a while. She had a comfy flat and I enjoyed exploring London. I was embracing the hippie lifestyle. Greece had recently been in the news as a hippie destination. The Matala Caves were on the southern part of the island of Crete. They have a long history, dating back to the Neolithic times. It is believed they were originally used as tombs during the Roman occupation over two-thousand years ago.

"Hippie backpackers came from all over the globe to dwell in what was once a quiet Greek island town. Since places to live were scarce, the flower children took refuge in the caves above Matala Beach.

It must have been the clear blue waters of the Mediterranean Sea and starry moonlight sky that drew them in. It was truly a place where they could disconnect and express themselves without judgment from the outside world.

The hippie caves most famous resident was singer/songwriter Joni Mitchell who immortalized the Matala Caves with her 1971 song "Carey."

According to Joni Mitchell, when they arrived in Matala Greece there was nothing more than two grocery stores and a bakery."

—"Getting Lost in the Hippie Caves of Matala Crete" *NothingFamiliar.com* by Brigitte & Jake

Greece was calling me, so after a couple of weeks in London, I flew to Athens, where I stayed for a few days, eating souvlaki and baklava. From there, I took a boat to Crete. Since it was already rumored that the church and military were unhappy with the hippies camping out in the caves, I found a room with a bathroom in a small fishing village. Breakfast was at one of the couple of tavernas in town. It took a few days to get used to eating the eggs fried in olive oil and the coffee so thick a spoon could just about stand up in the cup.

I made friends with one of the fishermen, who would bring in his catch and give me a fish for dinner. We would go to the grape vineyards, pick the snails off the walls and bring them to the taverna, where they would cook them into a beautiful stew with tomatoes and potatoes. There was a lot of dancing, Ouzo and plate breaking. I stayed in that wonderful town for a few weeks.

Then, I got the traveling fever again. I wanted to go east to Turkey and Morocco. However, I knew that a woman traveling alone would not be a good idea, so I went to the local Youth Hostile looking for a traveling companion.

That's when I met Pierre and my life changed forever. He was another hippie from France. He told me his plans to get a VW bus in Athens and travel east. He seemed nice enough, so I agreed to be his traveling companion. A couple of days later, we got on the boat back to Athens. It was crowded with people, chickens and goats and seemed to take forever. When we got to Athens, we got a hotel room with two beds. The plan was to stay there until we secured a vehicle and then travel east.

As we were settling into our room, Pierre suddenly changed his attitude. Out of nowhere, he grabbed me, put my arm behind my back, and started pulling off my clothes. I tried to say *no* to no avail. I had no idea how to fight back or resist. I had never before experienced any violence in my life. I decided not to resist and just give in. I remember lying there like a dead fish while he violated me. When he was finished, he began to declare his love for me. He said we would have a wonderful life together. I thought he had absolutely no grip on the reality of the situation. Fortunately, he fell asleep. This gave me the opportunity to get dressed, gather my things and quietly escape. I had one friend who lived in the basement of his parents' home. I went there and told him what happened. I was afraid Pierre would be looking for me, so I hid there for a few days. This was my first experience with rape that would begin to shape my future life.

I stayed in Greece, island hopping for a few more days, then took a train through Yugoslavia to Austria. It was 1972, so Yugoslavia had not yet become Serbia and Montenegro. Since I was born in Vienna, I knew I wanted to explore that city. I found the people cold and unfriendly. Walking around the city after dark, I was often approached by men who thought I was a street walker (prostitute). The best thing there was the pastries.

I continued my European adventure in Innsbruck and Salzburg, which I found stunningly beautiful. Then, onto Italy, where I traveled through Rome, Venice, Naples, Capri and Florence with my mother who met me there, so we could spend a couple of weeks together. I remember sitting at an outdoor restaurant in Naples that was by the water. Gypsy boys would swim up and try to grab women's pocketbooks if they were within reach on a lap or hanging on the back of a chair.

While in Capri we visited the amazing Blue Grotto. This is a sea cave where you ride on a rowboat and must lean back, in order to fit through the cave mouth to enter. The very small entrance forces the skipper to bring in his oars, as well. Once inside, the amazing blue water is a spectacular sight. We also visited the glass blowing Murano factory. I still have a beautiful vase and two fish from that visit. Then, it was on to Paris for a few days and finally back to London. After over five months of traveling around Europe, I returned to home to New York.

Italy, 1971

Chapter Nine
Moving to Woodstock

Being back in NYC at my parents' home at 23 years old was a culture shock. I decided to look for a job out of the city. The Village Voice was the best newspaper to search for a job that was offbeat and not in an office. I found an ad placed by a couple who lived in Greenwich Village during the week and went to their home in Woodstock, NY on the weekends. They were looking for someone to take care of their home and pool during the week and watch their little girl on the weekends. This was perfect for me. I packed up my VW Bug and moved into their country home. It was a great summer job, so I decided to look for something more permanent there, after it ended.

I found a studio apartment in a large farmhouse that had been renovated and broken up into individual studios. Woodstock was just a small upstate town at the time. It had a few mom and pop stores and a couple of cafes. Unfortunately, it has now become a big tourist attraction with overpriced, fancy stores.

I took a job as a waitress at the Bear Cafe that was owned by Albert Grossman, who lived nearby in Bearsville. He was a record producer and manager for many famous artists of that time, including Bonnie Raitt, Paul Butterfield, The Band, Janis Joplin, Maria Muldaur, Peter, Paul and Mary, David Sanborn and Todd Rundgren. Grossman had also been Bob Dylan's manager for years. He owned quite a bit of property in Bearsville, including his home, a recording studio, the Bear Cafe and the Bear Restaurant. He was a somewhat unapproachable individual, with a stern air about him.

My direct boss was Maggie Denver, divorced from Bob Denver of *Gilligan's Island* fame. She was about ten years older than me, with two children. We became good friends and she was a cool role model. It was not unusual to come to work and serve various members of The Band, who were regulars there. I worked at the Cafe for close to two years, eventually becoming the night manager, until it closed for financial reasons. It was a great time, meeting many new people, living a carefree life.

While working there, I also did some house-sitting for Paul Butterfield. He lived in a grand home, a few miles outside of town. He had a blues band that would go touring. I recall Gene Dinwiddie playing with him at the time. The last time I ever drank Tequila was in that house. Exactly what occurred that evening, I'm not sure but I do know it convinced me that Tequila is not a good drink for me! I vaguely remember a night when Dr. John was hitting the keys. Sadly, Butterfield died of an accidental overdose in 1987. Another great talent lost too soon.

During that time, I moved again. This time, it was to the red house across from the Millstream on the bottom of O'Hayo Mountain Road. It was just down the hill from Bob Dylan's house but I never saw him. He was quite a recluse. My father had always wanted to buy a house in the Catskills and since I was already living there, I suggested Woodstock. If he would buy it, I would gladly pay the monthly mortgage to live there. The house was right outside of town.

It was a 1905 two-story, craftsman-style cottage with a main room, eat-in kitchen—with a large pantry—and small bathroom on the ground floor, and two bedrooms and a bathroom upstairs. The bedroom windows faced the road and stream. The little waterfall could be heard all night from my window. There was a fireplace in the main room, which we later switched to a more efficient wood-burning stove. The woodwork was beautifully maintained and surrounded the many windows in the main room. A sizable porch was later screened in for summer nights. Every Spring, the large lilac bush out front would bloom, releasing its perfume throughout the house. Only one house was near us and my friend Serge lived there. He was the local pot dealer, which made my life even better. I remember thinking I wanted to grow old in that house.

The Woodstock House With Our Zujitsu Family

Chapter Ten
Back to NYC

After the Bear Cafe closed, I waitressed at a couple of other places in town. However, when the New York Shakespeare Company arrived at the Byrdcliffe Center for the 1974 summer, I decided to pursue my interest in the theater. After all, theater had been my minor in college. I got a job, working backstage for that summer and then moved back to New York City in the Fall to pursue another theater gig.

My next job was producer's assistant for a show called *What's A Nice Country Like You Doing in a State Like This?* The producer, Bud Friedman was also the owner of the well-known comedy club, called The Improv. It was a great show but like all shows, it eventually closed and I was out on unemployment, again. My final theater gig was working the props for Shakespeare in the Park, an annual summer event, held at the Delacorte Theater in Central Park. Our home base was at the Public Theater on Astor Place. At that time, it was being run by the founder, Joseph Papp. These shows were free and very popular, with folks lining up for hours to get tickets.

When I found myself again on the unemployment line after that summer, I decided I just didn't love the work enough to live the uncertain lifestyle. It was time to find something different and something different found me. My parents had a close friend, who was the director of a laboratory in Mt. Sinai Hospital in Manhattan. Apparently, there was an on-the-job training program that paid two-hundred dollars a week (in 1975 a somewhat decent salary). After six months, I could take an exam, certifying me as a Chemistry Laboratory Technician with full benefits and better salary. The hospital, located on the Upper East Side of Manhattan, was convenient to drive my VW bug from my Brownstone apartment on East 6th Street. Although I really did not like the job at all, I liked the flexible schedule that allowed me to pursue my other interests. I ended up working in that laboratory from 1975 until 1987.

Chapter Eleven
My Martial Arts Life Begins

I also joined a nearby gym, called the New York Health and Racquet Club, where I could take yoga and calisthenics classes and strength train. At that time, there were no Aerobics classes yet. As it turned out, a karate class was scheduled before my calisthenics class, so I often would be there early to watch. The karate class was run by someone named Wilfredo Roldan—a second-degree black belt in Nisei Goju Karate—whom they called "Sensei," the Japanese word for teacher. I watched class a few times before I joined. I had recently been abused by a former boyfriend and decided this would be a good skill to learn.

So, I began my search for a teacher and style that fit me. I had no idea martial arts would become a lifelong journey. Karate training was unlike any other I had ever experienced. Even though classes were in a health club, they were sometimes quite extreme. Between his street-like attitude and the severe training he had experienced, Roldan's teaching methods were often quite rough and crude. As part of our training, he would put each student in a chokehold until they passed out. I was already very fit, so the physical challenges were not a big deal. However, sparring was a different story. This was not something that came easily but I persevered.

At my first karate tournament, I actually won first place in kumite (sparring)—my very first medal. After achieving green belt, the reward was to go train at the Nisei Goju Headquarters in the East Village at the University of the Streets. This is where Frank Ruiz—Nisei founder—lived and taught. He was a former U.S. Marine, who had been awarded a Purple Heart, Bronze Star and

Silver Star and he was the senior student of legendary Peter Urban. He used to say, "I'm the baddest mther-fkr around," which was evidenced by the amazing group of men who became his students. Men like Ron Van Clief, Louis Delgado, Malachi Lee, Herbie Thompson, Tom "La Puppet" Caroll, and Chaka Zulu—were all well-known, as champions in the martial arts world.

Training at the main dojo was intense. Most days, I would put on a bunch of protective equipment and then spar with everyone there, until I was too exhausted to continue. Fortunately, although the protective equipment was heavy, it protected me from serious injury. I left Nisei Goju before testing for my purple belt (for personal reasons), looking for a more traditional style.

In late 1978, I joined the Kyokushin Karate dojo on Wooster Street, led by Nobuyuki Kishi, a fifth-degree black belt under legendary karate master, Mas Oyama—known for killing bulls. I still treasure my first Kyu brown-belt certificate, signed by Mas Oyama when he visited our dojo. I remember the class, standing downstairs on the street, barefoot, in uniform, waiting for his arrival. Kishi's favorite demo was breaking baseball bats with his shin kick. He would spend hours shin kicking the heavy bag, desensitizing his legs.

All classes were exactly the same format: basics, kata, two-step self-defenses and finally, sparring. However, this sparring was different. No protective equipment was allowed and training was on a wood floor. I was often paired off to spar with Frank, a brown belt built like a tank. High roundhouse kicks were my favorite but he would catch my kick and sweep me, dumping me to the floor. Kishi never taught us falling skills, so being swept was always painful. During testing for first Kyu brown belt, unfortunately, I sustained a serious broken finger requiring surgery. Although I loved martial arts training, I felt that the Kyokushin style was not right for me. My search for the right style and teacher was not over.

**First Place Medal for
Kumite (Sparring), 1977**

Chapter Twelve
Meeting Chaka Zulu

At the end of December 1980, a neighbor invited me to a party at a dojo on Second Avenue between 5th Street and 6th Street. It was a birthday celebration for a few Capricorns, including the man who had the dojo. His name was Chaka Zulu, a fifth-degree black belt in Nisei Goju Karate. His dojo was quite well known, as there were few dojos in Manhattan at the time—not like now, with one on every street. It was a loft space on the second floor of a building on Second Avenue between 5th Street and 6th Street. I had previously seen him at a tournament, where he performed with various weapons to music. This was before musical forms, when there were mostly only sparring and forms divisions in tournaments. I also knew he was in the 1975 documentary *The Warrior Within*.

I remember our first meeting, when I arrived at the party. He was so charming. When I reached out to shake his hand, he took it and kissed it, old-fashioned style. It was a great party and I thought no more of it, until a couple of months later, when I was completing my Masters Degree in Physical Education at NYU. My thesis required I visit karate schools to interview the instructors and have the students complete questionnaires. I called several instructors I knew including Zulu, Toyotaro Miyazaki, Kishi and others. I was glad when Zulu agreed to participate. I was to interview him the next afternoon, in between classes. As I walked through the door, on the left, were the large windows on the avenue with hanging plants, and chairs for visitors/spectators. The workout area was carpeted and one long wall was all exposed brick. Beyond, were dressing areas, restroom, heavy bag and weapons. Zulu had also built an area for his dog, complete with fire hydrant. There also was a "black belt only" private area in back where Zulu lived.

At the interview, he invited me to bring my uniform and try a class. I did and was amazed. They were not only kicking and punching but they were falling, rolling, ground-fighting, throwing and defending against multiple opponents. There was also great music being played in the background. Since I was so close to achieving my black belt in Kyokushin, leaving was a difficult decision. However, after a few weeks of going to both schools, I made my choice and joined Chaka Zulu's School of Karate in March 1981.

During the '80s, martial arts schools were clearly dominated by men. Few women were training and many schools had none or only a handful of women. Often, male instructors would send the females to the side to practice forms and little else. It was common for women to leave some schools, complaining that they were not receiving adequate training. This was not the case at Zulu's dojo. As a matter of fact, he has always said he loves to train women because they come in without preconceived notions of fighting or using their muscular strength. Instead, they tend to focus on perfecting the techniques. The women and men in the dojo were treated the same. With my previous experience, it only took me another year to get my black belt. I had finally found my martial arts home.

That first year was a real challenge. Not only did I have to learn new physical skills but I also had to deal with being the "new kid on the block." Zulu did not believe in taking away rank achieved in another karate system. He did not want "a ringer" in his class wearing a white belt, so he allowed me to wear my brown belt. This presented some competitive situations with the other female brown belt—his girlfriend at the time. I remember the first time we two women were required to spar. I had been training in a dojo with traditional etiquette and rules, so when my hair was pulled during the fight, I really didn't know how to respond. However, it didn't take long to adapt and appreciate this more realistic training.

That next summer of '81, one of the students had a party at her house. Apparently, Zulu—now single—had already been attracted to me but had not acted on it, until then. I was pleasantly surprised at his romantic interest. Soon after, we arranged a secret meeting. I was to pick him up, as he waited in front of a church, a few blocks away and take him to Queens, where I was living. In the beginning, neither of us wished to have our connection made public. As life would have it, we fell in love and have been together ever since. Unfortunately, Chaka lost this dojo space a few months later, when the building was sold to a developer, who wanted to more than triple the rent. When a friend of ours decided to move to New Mexico, we got his apartment and moved in, together. It was a small one-bedroom on the fourth floor of a Brownstone on 88th Street between York Avenue and East End Avenue in Manhattan.

When I was a young Hippie in the '70s, I thought that Racism was on its way out. I believed in my young generation, that promoted love, peace and equality. These older, racist people would not prevail and would just die off. Martin Luther's dream for his four little children would come true—they would "live in a nation where they will not be judged by the color of their skin but by the content of their character." I wanted to believe it, so I did. To me, everyone had the potential to be a "good person" or a "bad person", regardless of their skin color.

I only dated White men until my mid twenties. It was really for no other reason than the opportunity never arose. Most of the places I went and the friends I had were White. I just didn't meet any Latino or Black men to date, until I started working at Mt. Sinai Hospital. It is a large hospital, like a small city. Every December, a huge holiday party would be held in the expansive main lobby. It was a glorious affair with great food and a fantastic DJ. Those were some of the best holiday parties I ever attended.

I met Ricardo at the 1978 party. He was a Black Cuban who worked in another department at the hospital. Ricardo was tall, slim and athletic. He was also a third-degree black belt in Shotokan Karate. Rick was a great salsa dancer and would take me to the clubs in the Bronx and teach me how to salsa. I always loved to dance and it was so fun. Growing up in Cuba, his Black experience was much different than if he had grown up in Harlem. He was grateful to be in the U.S. He was easy-going and fun-loving. We would take rides upstate to enjoy the greenery, while singing along with the tunes on the radio. We would search through thrift stores and play paddleball at the nearby courts. I would cook him a steak, rice and banana dinner at my apartment on Houston and Mott Street. We dated for nearly a year.

I was nearly thirty years old then but had no desire or thoughts about marriage or children. Growing up as an only child, I didn't really understand the concept of a large family. After my early failed marriage, I had no desire to try it again. I was satisfied training Karate, working at Mt. Sinai, studying for my Physical Education Masters Degree at NYU, and dating. Until I met Chaka Zulu.

The best thing to hold onto in life is each other.

\- Audrey Hepburn

Stand for something or you will fall for anything.

\- Rosa Parks

Happiness often sneaks in through a door you didn't know you left open.

\- John Barrymore

They say age is just a number, but to me, it's a collection of memories that can never be erased.

\- Joan Baez

Part Three

Our Life Together

Chapter One
Black & White Together

Oxford dictionary defines *microaggression* as a "statement, action, or incident regarded as an instance of indirect, subtle, or unintentional discrimination against members of a marginalized group such as a racial or ethnic minority." According to the Cleveland Clinic, "their impact is anything but small." Some examples are: "Can I touch your hair?" "You don't act like other gays." "That's so ghetto." "You speak English quite well." "I have many Black friends." "I don't see color." This last one speaks volumes to me. I always believed that when I said that I don't see color, that was a good thing. It meant I was not a racist, that I believed everyone was equal. However, that's really not the case.

It is important that we all acknowledge that Non-White folks are not treated the same as White folks. It's called "White Privilege," a term that many White people do not understand or believe in. It's as simple as understanding that when two people enter a store, one White and one Non-White, the White person will get acknowledged and served first, while the Non-White person will have a security guard follow them around to make sure they don't steal anything.

This treatment has become much more apparent to me during my relationship with Chaka. Over the years, we have experienced far more incidents of microaggression than overt macro-aggression. I know that many incidents of microaggression have not even been acknowledged by me because they are so subtle. However, Chaka always recognizes them and—as each one adds more fuel to the fire—the experiences have placed a great, painful burden on him.

For me, the most painful experience of microaggression was the refusal of my parents to ever meet Chaka. For the first couple of years we lived together, I didn't even speak to them because whenever I called, they would give me grief about my relationship with Chaka. My father insisted he was not racist because he had colleagues and students who were Black. However, having an interracial, intimate relationship was not the same and they would not condone it.

My mother went along with his opinion, although I'm sure she would have been accepting. I understood that she needed to go along with her husband's decision. When we were alone she told me her biggest fear was that I would have a hard life being in an interracial relationship and she only wanted the best for me. It was painful for me to disassociate myself from them during that time.

After a couple of years, I resumed my relationship with my parents with the understanding that we would never speak of it again. Their attitude was always difficult for me to understand, given the fact that they were Holocaust survivors and had been persecuted solely for the fact they were Jewish. Their attitude toward my chosen partner seemed no different than the attitude of their persecutors. It was very painful for me but it didn't change my mind. In fact, it made me more resolute.

Over the years, Chaka and I have also experienced several overt incidents of macro-aggression. One Saturday morning in the early 1980s, as we were driving on the New York State Thruway—up to the cottage in the Catskills that we had purchased—we were pulled over by a State Trooper. At the time, I was driving our Ford Pinto, a car that barely could go the 65 MPH speed limit. After he confirmed my license and registration, he directed us to get out of the car. Then, he had Chaka put his hands up on the car and spread his legs so he could search him. Next, he had us open the trunk for another search but found nothing. I was torn between being angry and scared but I said to him, "We did nothing wrong. You stopped us because I'm White and he is Black." My honesty surprised him and he insisted we were stopped because our car fit the description of a stolen vehicle. Finally, he told us to sign a statement that we consented to his search! We just wanted to get going, so we signed it.

Another incident with the law, occurred in 2015. We had already moved out of New York but came for a visit to see family and conduct some classes with our martial arts students. It was a warm, August evening. We had been teaching a class at our Manhattan dojo where two of our senior black belts were teaching. After class, everyone went for sushi at a nearby restaurant. We were staying at our black belt Eric's home in Brooklyn and we were in his car. The windows were rolled down in the ten-year-old Mercedes. Eric was driving, Chaka was in the front seat and I was in the back seat. As we were stopped at a red light, seemingly out of nowhere, we were surrounded by three policemen with their hands on their revolvers. One asked Eric for his license and registration. Another came close to look at Chaka and me in the back. As a former U.S. Marine, Chaka always wears a cap indicating he is a USMC Veteran. That most likely impressed the officer and I appeared just fine in the back seat. Fortunately, they just let us go without any further incident but I was clearly freaked out.

After both of these occurrences—and especially after the unsolicited killings of Black people by the police in recent years—I will never call the police for "help," if Chaka is with me.

Incidents of macro-aggression are particularly egregious when they occur with friends or at their homes. Early on in our relationship, we attended a small gathering at the home of Chaka's friends. Upon entering, I noticed that I was the only White person there. It should have not been an issue but I was immediately uncomfortable. At one point, I found myself in the living room with all the women, while Chaka was in the bedroom with the men. Although I tried to be friendly, I did not feel welcomed by these women, so I decided to go into the bedroom to be closer to Chaka. I walked in and tried to hint to him that I was not feeling comfortable, when one of the men approached me. He began questioning me, saying, "What are you doing here? You're strange. You don't belong here." Chaka looked at him and was about to explode when Jimmy—the party host—heard him and immediately came to my defense. He told him I was Chaka's wife. He said, "Chaka is a fifth degree black belt and if you don't apologize, all I can do for you is call the ambulance." He backed off and that was the end of it but the arrow had already pierced me.

The next hurtful incident occurred when we traveled to St. Thomas, USVI. This is where Chaka's mother grew up, where he still had many family members and students and he visited quite often. We were staying at his auntie's home. It was 1982 and there were very few interracial couples there in those days. I felt many eyes staring at us, when we walked Main Street. One day, we went to the local barber shop, owned by one of Chaka's friends. It was a hangout for some of the guys, as often are barber shops. I did not feel welcomed there but stayed quiet, as the men gossiped and bantered. As we were leaving, we heard the owner say, "Why did he bring that White woman here?" His words pierced us both.

I did not return to St. Thomas for nearly twenty years. When I did return in 2001, many things had changed. Now, there were many more interracial couples and I felt much more comfortable and welcomed. Indeed, we ended up purchasing the condo on the Sapphire Beach marina. We spent many wonderful times there and made some good friends—both White and Black. In 2021, we sold it when the market was strong and we had moved to California.

We have taken two cruises to Alaska and about a half-dozen cruises to various places, including the Eastern Caribbean, Western Caribbean, Panama Canal and Mediterranean. Our very first cruise to the Eastern Caribbean, was on Royal Caribbean Cruise Line. At the time, the Voyager of the Seas was the largest cruise ship ever built. It had every amenity one could imagine. The main corridor was like Bourbon Street in the French Quarter of New Orleans. It was vibrant, colorful and festive. The ship even had an ice skating rink!

One evening, we went to see an ice skating performance. As we took our seats, just before the performance began, we heard a woman sitting behind us, speaking to her friend. "Oh my God! Can you imagine waking up to see his Black face every morning? How disgusting." Then the lights dimmed and the performance began. When it was over, before we could turn around to confront her, she had rushed out. But the damage was done. Her cruelty had hit us hard. Fortunately, we didn't see her for the rest of our voyage.

In 2000, after my parents passed away, we inherited the house in Woodstock. It was located right across the Millstream waterfall where many locals came to swim and hangout. Sometimes, on the weekends, tourists would come and park in our driveway or on the road. Since the road was somewhat narrow and on a curve, it was quite dangerous to park there. One Saturday, a family from out of town, parked their car right on the curve where someone driving down the hill could easily have hit it. I came out of our house and shouted to the man, that parking there was very dangerous and he should really move his car. Even though I spoke very politely, he immediately became defensive and somewhat belligerent. When Chaka heard this, he came out to reinforce my warning that this was a dangerous place to park. After a few words were exchanged, this guy said to Chaka, "You people...". He was obviously referring to Chaka being Black. This conversation did not have to go that way but he chose to make it a racist issue. They eventually left.

We moved to California in 2017, just six miles east of Laguna Beach. One evening, our neighbor told us about the annual Art Walk. Laguna Beach is a big tourist destination with races of many people, represented. There are many art galleries on the main drag and once a year for a week, all the galleries are open to the public in the evening. A free trolley drives up and down the mile-long street where you can get off at any stop to check out the galleries. Most galleries are just one large room but this one had three different rooms of art hanging on the walls. Chaka and I walked in and began looking around. At one point, we got separated. I noticed as Chaka was looking at the artwork, the security guard began to follow him. After a short time, it became obvious the guard was tailing him, so Chaka decided to just sit down on one of the benches. Later, he told me that instead of having the security guard continue to follow him, he decided to just sit down and wait for me. It was obvious and quite ridiculous. *Did he really think Chaka was going to steal a painting off the wall?*

Then, there are the numerous incidents that occurred at various restaurants. On our way home from a visit to Maine, we stopped at a Friendly's Restaurant. We sat down at a booth and waited for our waitress. Well we waited and waited and she finally came over with the menus. Then, we waited and waited for her to take our order. When our food finally arrived, she basically threw our plates down on the table. We made sure to inspect our food carefully to ensure it had not been spit on or thrown on the floor or such. Needless to say, we left her three pennies in the shape of Mickey Mouse as her tip. That was our last visit to any Friendly's Restaurant—not very friendly!

One late afternoon, when we were living in Forest Hills, Queens, we decided to go to our favorite Japanese restaurant and sit at the hibachi table. As we sat there sipping our sake, two women came into the restaurant. They decided to sit at the hibachi table and took seats on the far end of the table, perpendicular to us. We immediately felt them staring at us, as one of the women clutched her handbag. They were quite far from us but continued to give us *dirty looks* during the entire meal. They finished their meal before us, gathered their things and began to walk toward the door. This is when I noticed a briefcase that one of the women forgot, which was still on the bench near us. I stopped them and said, "Don't forget your briefcase." Needless to say, they were startled and embarrassed—and thankful. Sometimes Karma is instant!

These are just a few of the micro and macro aggressions we have encountered during the years. My temperament has mostly allowed me to create a hard shell around my emotions. However, my dear husband—who has endured racist attitudes all his life—is much more sensitive to it all.

Chapter Two
Early Years on 88th Street

Zosia and Chaka, 1982

For our first ten years together—1982-1992—we lived in the fourth floor walk-up building on 88th Street, right down the block from the New York Mayor's mansion and the East River. We were still relatively young, so walking up and down the stairs with groceries, laundry and our martial arts gear kept us in fit shape. The apartment was always dark—with only one small window in the living room and adjoining tiny kitchen—and it looked out to an air shaft. The bedroom had a decent window with a fire escape, so it always needed to be locked. In order to get to the bathroom, you had to walk through the bedroom. But it was our home.

Chaka's main source of income for many years had been the dojo. Since it was also where he lived, it was affordable. However, with apartment rent and dojo space rental, finances became tight. In 1983, I was excited when I secured an adjunct teaching position at Adelphi University, teaching self-defense. I also still worked my lab technician position at Mt. Sinai until 1987, when I quit and began a full-time fitness career.

Meanwhile, Chaka took on a day job as a youth counselor for troubled young men. He ended up working for two well known groups. Although all the young men respected and listened to him, the administration was not *on board* and would give him a hard time. They were trained on paper, while Chaka had been trained by the school of hard knocks.

S.T. '96 TRAINERS N.W.M.A.F.

1996 Trainers at the National Women's Martial Arts Federation Training

Chapter Three
Meeting My Tribe of Sister Warriors

History shows us that there have been many female warriors throughout time. According to Robin Cross and Rosalind Miles in their book *Warrior Women: 3000 Years of Courage and Heroism*, many women fought on the front lines and were leaders of great armies. The Amazons were likely the very first female tribe —originally in Libya—where drawings as far back as 2000 BC have been discovered. The women were often pictured on horseback, fighting with bows and arrows. There have been many stories written and verbally passed down for years about their tribe. It is said they lived and fought together, never marrying but using men to have babies, only keeping the females and discarding the males. Indeed, the popular TV series, *Xena* is based on Amazonian legends.

In Vietnam, a proverb is attributed to the two Trung sister warriors who led a rebellion against the Chinese Han Dynasty: "When war comes, even women have to fight." Just about every country's history includes a female warrior, who was a leader in battle. Some of the most effective Japanese ninja spies were women who were able to use trickery and feminine wiles to discover secrets to lure men to their deaths. In America, one of the bravest and most well known female fighters, was a Black woman named Harriet Ross Tubman. Born into slavery in 1820 in Maryland, she led over seventy slaves through the Underground Railroad to freedom and became a spy in the Union Army.

For those readers who are not martial artists, it usually takes between four and eight years to achieve a black belt in one style. It is usually dependent on the school, the style and how many hours of training per week one devotes. There are also several colored belts before achieving black belt. Everyone begins as a white belt. The most common order is white, yellow, blue, orange, green, purple, brown and then black. Some styles do not use all the colors. Then there are ten degrees of black belt. Many more years are required to advance the degrees of black belt. The main styles of martial arts are karate, tae kwon do, jujitsu, judo, aikido, kung fu, arnis/kali and modern eclectic. The arts of Tai Chi and Qi Gong are considered *internal* arts and usually do not use a belt system. There are also numerous systems in each style, developed by various masters throughout history. All, except one system, developed by men. That one system is Wing Chun Kung Fu, created by the Shaolin nun, Ng Mui in the seventeenth century.

Martial arts in America have always been dominated by men. When I began training in 1976, there were very few other women training. There were a couple of women in Chaka Zulu's school but no one much more advanced than me. The only woman I knew who was a black belt and had her own school, was Elba "Cookie" Melendez. Her dojo, The Shotokan Karate Studio, established in 1980, was near us in the East Village of New York. She was also NY's first Female World Kickboxing Champion and a real pioneer. Meeting her was a highlight for me and we are still friends.

In the spring of 1982—now a young black belt at thirty-three years old—I heard about a women's martial arts camp that summer, called Special Training. For the past six years, my training had been mostly with men, so an all-women's camp sounded exciting. It was to be held in Provincetown, Massachusetts, organized by the National Women's Martial Arts Federation, a fairly new organization. At this camp, there would be many female black belts and an all-female teaching staff.

So, I piled into my car with my dojo sisters and drove to camp. We all stayed at the local Holiday Inn motel, ate the all-included meals at the Chinese Restaurant—including egg foo yung for breakfast—and trained all over town, including the beach, the park and the town hall. There were three-hundred, seventy-five women in attendance, representing various martial arts. The teachers were outstanding, : Bobbi Snyder (RIP) Okinawan Shorin-Ryu Karate, Chief Instructor of the Feminist Karate Union in Pittsburgh, Pennsylvania—Master Bow-Sim Mark, president of the Chinese Wu-Shu Research Institute in Boston and mother of Donnie Yen, famed kung fu movie star—Jaye Spiro, from her Shotokan Karate Dojo in Detroit—Wendi Dragonfire, Shuri Ryu Karate head instructor of Valley Women's Martial Arts in Springfield, Massachusetts, who now resides in Holland—Lynette Love, future Tae Kwon Do 1984 Olympic teammate from Detroit—Barbara Bones, Kajukenbo tournament fighter and head instructor for Amazon Kung Fu, a collective school in Eugene, Oregon, who now lives in Hawaii—Cassandra George, co-director of Wind and Water Martial Arts, from upstate New York—and several other impressive female martial artists.

These were women I had just read about in Black Belt Magazine. Many were my age but had been training for twice my six years. They were top competitors on the tournament circuit, most owning their own schools. I was so excited to be training with them. I drank up every moment. The environment was extremely supportive. Indeed, I am still friends with most of these women. Jaye Spiro and I still reminisce about her knife defense class. Driving back to the city, I declared that Special Training was one of the best experiences of my life. This event marks the real beginning of my Sister Warrior Tribe of women martial artists, that now numbers well over two-hundred women.

Who are my tribal sister warriors? We represent all shades of skin color. We are White (Caucasian), Black, Latina, Asian and all mixes. We live throughout the United States, Canada, Bermuda, Holland, Germany, Mexico, Israel, Vietnam and beyond. We are Christian, Jewish, Muslim, Buddhist and Atheist. We are physical therapists, teachers, acupuncturists, lawyers, social workers, fitness instructors, IT *peeps*, travel agents, veterinarians, martial arts instructors and more. What we all have in common, is our love for the martial arts, exhibited by our devotion to training for at least twenty to more than fifty years. We also believe that women should be in charge of their own bodies and have the right to defend themselves.

2023 Association of Women Martial Arts Instructors Conference Staff

Chapter Four
The Art of Zujitsu-Ryu is Born
As told by its founder, Chaka Zulu

By 1984, it was clear to me and our black belts that what I was teaching was no longer the second-generation Japanese style of Nisei Goju. Yes, we still kept many of the basics but that's where it ended. Our training now included elements of Judo, Jujitsu, Marine Corps training, Tae Kwon Do and most of all, unique drills and exercises that were exclusively created by me. We would now be Zujitsu Martial Arts, combining the "Zu" of Zulu with "jitsu" meaning art, or The Art of Zulu.

One of my greatest joys was seeing my teacher, Frank Ruiz, wearing a sweatshirt with my new Zujitsu logo and receiving his blessing. Unfortunately, diabetes got the best of Ruiz and before he passed in 1995, he was in a wheelchair with his legs amputated below his knees.

I recall a very funny situation that happened in St. Croix when I went to a tournament. Ruiz was already there and we were picked up at the airport. We all walked into the yard where he was sitting in his wheelchair at the end of porch, several yards away. When I walked in the gate and saw him there, I said, "You know, I oughta kick your f-kin ass!" Well, everyone broke out in hysterical laughter. Ruiz was laughing so hard he nearly fell out of his chair. I was so far away from him that it was hilarious and even then, I was scared to death. It was one of the last times I saw him.

My martial arts philosophy has been molded by all my life experiences. *He who cannot defend himself owns nothing, not good fortune or even his own life.* You should not start out from a weak point in an attack. To me, a weak point means if someone attacks me with a knife and I say, "I'm just going to control him or disarm him." No. That's not my attitude. My attitude is, "I'm going to kill you! If I see you can't handle what I've got, I will de-escalate. But there's no way I'm going to rev myself up from that low point of control to, "I'm going to kill you." It's not going to happen that way. And it's going to take too long to get there. So, I must start from the top first. I'm going to kill you and if I don't have to, I won't but I'm not going to start from the weak point, first. That makes no sense to me and it may cause me to lose my life.

The problem is, the majority of the people you are going to have in your school probably never had a fight in their entire life. They don't know what it is to be hit or what it is to hit somebody. In the process of your teaching, you must try to impart that to your student, without injuring or damaging them. This is one of the reasons (why), when I lay my hands on my students, I lay them on heavy. I know how much control I have. *I'm not going to injure you but I'm going to make you feel something you need to feel.* In a real fight, it's going to be worse than that—guaranteed.

Even though I might teach my students the same techniques or concepts, I expect them to grasp them differently, simply because they are different people. That allows me to learn new things based on what I gave them. If everyone in the dojo was doing the exact same thing, how could I learn anything from them? I mean, they can learn from me because I've been training the longest but I wouldn't learn anything from them. I would remain stagnant and that would be a waste of my time. So, based on what I do and the way I teach, I get so much from my students, that I never get bored. The training and the knowledge is absolutely endless because everyone is grasping what I'm doing in a different way.

What I see in most schools and systems is—two guys walk in and one guy can do a split and the other guy can't. So the guy who can't is ignored and all (the students) see is the other guy's trophies. That's wrong, because this guy can be as deadly as the other guy. It depends who's teaching them. In my opinion, the problem is that most people don't see teaching as an art. They are just repeating what they learned but teaching is an art in itself.

In traditional karate, after the students learn kicks, they practice defenses against kicks—all kinds of defenses against kicks. I don't teach like that because I don't want my students to wait for some specific attack that may never come. When you're looking for that foot to come and a punch sneaks in instead and hits you in the nose, you've been looking for the wrong thing. I condition my students to accept whatever comes first. A fist, a punch, an elbow, a knee, doesn't make any difference. You deal with whatever attacks you first. If you condition yourself to look for that leg to come because he has long legs, you might miss that punch. I teach differently.

I don't know how to explain that other than, if my students are trapped in a bathroom stall with a guy wielding a straight razor or a knife, there's no room to kick, punch, throw or any of that. I want them to be able to manipulate this individual's knife so that he carves himself up with his own weapon. That takes a different kind of training that I have not yet seen in this country, except in my system because I know what I want for me. That is what I pass on to my students. I want my students to be able to fight under any conditions and any type of opponent imaginable on the planet. That takes a certain kind of training—the ability to adapt and adjust in a split second.

Most people don't teach like that—they're developing clones. That's usually how it is in a traditional school—and I'm not putting down traditional schools—but for me, it's not good. I've been through it, so I know. There are often fallacies left in the students' heads:

One is the assumption that, if they get in a fight, they're going to have plenty of room to do it in.

Two: If they get in a fight, they're going to be able to see who they are fighting.

Three: If they get in a fight, it's only going to be with one individual.

Four: That (one) individual will have no skills.

Those are absolutely false beliefs but are in the students' heads almost automatically. This is because many instructors have accepted what they have gotten from their teacher but never analyzed it. If there are any flaws, they are passed along. *Not me.* I expect my students to analyze and tear down everything I give them. In order to be creative and adapt to who they are, they must.

The more you move, the more you can see. When a dance choreographer creates a dance, they don't sit at a table and write out the steps. They dance, start moving and within the movement, they start creating. The same principle applies to martial arts. If you're standing in one spot and fighting multiple opponents—first of all, you are the bullseye, that's going to be hit because you are stationery. Secondly, if you are in constant motion, you are less of a target. Thirdly, when in constant motion, you see various targets from different angles.

There are levels you go through in the martial arts, that one often does not realize. One of those levels is fear. It comes from the training, itself. At some point, you start to understand what you are capable of doing. You can break bricks and boards and it makes you realize what you can do to the human body. If you are a thinking individual, the first thing that has to result from (thinking), is fear. So, you start to tiptoe around society because you don't want to put yourself in a position of being forced to express yourself in that way and wind up in prison. Once you get past that point, the next level is the attitude that you're already dead. When you decide that death is no longer an issue, how can anybody hurt you? That attitude in itself emanates something others see, feel and stand back from.

Respect is of primary importance. We are teaching and learning dangerous stuff. No matter how high in skill or rank a person goes, they cannot demand or command respect. Respect has to be earned through tolerance, humility and self discipline. Without those qualities, it's just street fighting.

In most martial arts, a kick is a kick and a punch is a punch. What it amounts to, is: whoever is the biggest, fastest and strongest is going to be the winner. I'm not the biggest, fastest or strongest, so that doesn't guarantee me anything, unless I do something to offset what someone else is doing. That is what I do on a constant. I develop techniques that offset what they are doing —all the time. I don't have a choice about it. When working out with someone, the stronger they get, the softer I get. You don't know it but you're guiding me into hitting you because your muscle is telling me how to respond to you. As Mohammed Ali says, "Float like a butterfly, sting like a bee."

It's especially important for women to follow this principle instead of trying to compete with men by being stronger. That usually doesn't work and is a waste of energy. The concept of "softness" never registers in a strong man's head because he's been brought up to believe that strong muscles are everything. It's something but not everything. And what happens when you are eighty years old—what then? You should have been preparing for it long before you hit eighty.

Everything I have developed, comes out of my head and I can do it, instantly. My students have to practice and practice it until it becomes theirs. There are a lot of differences in what I teach because I have different ideas about what I want to do in a fight. I'm not going to allow other people to program me how to fight based on where they came from. I'm not a part of that, so I have to build things and fight based on the culture that surrounds me. I teach something different all the time. My head is constantly filled with all these creative ideas.

I may give you five self-defense techniques and then say to you, by next week I want you to turn them into fifteen. Now I force you to think and what comes out of that, will be with you forever. So my point is, when I take one technique, I automatically know it can be used in a thousand different ways. And because of that, it looks different every time but it's the same technique. You've got to let it happen in a fight situation, you have to train yourself to the point where you allow your instincts to work and let your training takeover.

I don't teach my students anything I don't demonstrate—of course, within limits of my eighty-six-year-old body. I want them to know (that) if I can do it, it can be done. I also want my students to remember that, if I'm teaching you something you can do, you've always got to know that it can be done to you. There has to be a counter to what you are doing. That's why you are training—to counter the next guy's thing. If you have two people that have serious skills, it could go on for days!

I guess the ultimate emphasis of what I'm trying to teach is absolute control of oneself. If you can control yourself, you can control the individuals around you. When I say control, I'm talking about physical control because I'm a martial artist. In the traditional concepts of martial arts, specifically karate, they do things like punch or kick at a candle and put out the flame with speed and force. To me, that is a semblance of control. There's nothing wrong with that but the kind of control I want, is the ability to take an opponent's attack and redirect it in such a way, that he has to come from the direction I dictate. And I should be there waiting for him! So, that means I took control of the situation and the attack, itself. That's control to me—manipulating people, bouncing them off walls at will—that's control. It's the kind of control I want.

The end result of this—aside from all the aesthetics, the meditation and the learning—is the fighting. Turn your body into a fighting machine. That comes first in my mind. Once I reach a level where I'm comfortable with that, then all the rest of the things can flow in without any problem because I have no fears about defending myself.

This is where I'm trying to get all my students. At some point, they will be eighty and ninety years old and that's when you are more vulnerable to assaults in this society. I don't care how old you are, I believe if you train right, you can overcome all of that. I am eighty-six years old now and still train six days a week. My training has changed but you can believe I am as deadly as ever.

"A Zujitsu-ka Must Be Gentle in Life, and Ferocious in Combat"

(A Zujitsu-ka is a student of Zujitsu)

For more information, please visit: Zujitsu.net

2018 Seminar at Bill McCloud's Brooklyn Dojo

Chapter Five

Dojo in the Woods
As told by Chaka Zulu

Of all the dojos we have trained in, my favorite was the Dojo in the Woods. This was an outdoor dojo at the cottage in the Catskill Mountains that we bought in 1983. It used to be part of an old colony where folks from New York City would spend their summers. The land was beautiful with many trees, a stream and a small lake nearby. I built thirty-nine training stations for the dojo. One weekend in that dojo, was like three months of training because of all of the devices. I created a map on wood for you to follow from one station to another. Zosia built a raised bed vegetable garden that was very prolific because of the great Spring and Summer climate. I had a small workshop where I could work on all my projects.

I built a solid wooden entry gate with an overhead sign, "Dojo in the Woods." As you entered, the first station was a giant wok filled with pebbles for iron palm and finger strengthening. There was a platform to practice katas (choreographed forms). We had an area for staff training where leather patches were secured to a tree at many different points as targets. Several striking bags were also suspended between trees.

Our neighbor there was an official at the airport and when he heard I was looking for a cargo net, he brought me one. The net was huge. I hung it up, tightly between a few trees. Then one day, when we were driving up from the city, we passed a big bag on the road. I had Zosia stop the car, so I could check it out. It was a big bag full of small, empty money bags. I took them up to the dojo, filled each one with sand, and hung them from the cargo net at different levels. I painted the one in the center, red. One of the drills was that all the other bags are trying to protect the red one. If I slapped one bag, it would touch another bag and move it, so now I had to worry about that bag. So, I must keep blocking and moving, trying to get to the red one. The other scenario was, I'm trying to protect the red bag from all the others. I secured another part of the cargo net to stakes about six inches off the ground. It created all these boxes. I would stand outside of the net with a long stick with a boxing glove at the end of it. I would be hitting you as you stepped in and out of the net, blocking the glove, trying not to fall.

A station called the Spider Web had five trees spanning about twelve feet with a large open area between them. I strung clothesline from tree to tree, everywhere, high and low. On the furthest tree, I hung a bell. The first time, you were required to go through the web with a small bowl of water without spilling it, hit the bell, and come back with the water. The second time, the bowl of water had a little leaf in it that you must not lose. The third time you went through with a staff. I used to bring my students to the front of the web and make them squat down. I'd say to them, because I had to learn this for myself in the Marine Corps, "Look, look through the Spider Web." Response, "O, dang Sensei, I see paths!" Yes, there are paths. All you have to do, is take your time and look. Same thing if you're going into the bush. You can't just run into the bush, blindly. This was a big learning experience.

I had one big tree and went up this tree myself to put in spikes, all the way up on both sides. The students had to climb up and down this tree. We also had three railroad ties that were elevated at different levels. You were required to practice on this narrow tie without falling. This balance work was used for weapons practice, kata and sparring. There were quite a few dummies built on several trees. One dummy's tongue would flop out if you didn't punch it right. Another dummy had strings and bungee cords that would slap you, if you slapped it wrong. We also had a pistol range where we could practice. A few of our students who were court officers would come up and help Zosia practice her firearm skills.

We had many wonderful weekends up there with students. When it was warm, we would go over to the lake for a swim. After a full day, we would have a big barbecue on our makeshift grill. I sliced an oil drum in half after thorough cleaning. Then, I put hinges on it, made holes for ventilation and got a big grate for the grill top. It became our go-to cooking venue. We kept that place well into the '90s and it will always be one of my favorite dojos.

**Chaka Sitting in Front of the
Dojo in the Woods Entrance**

Chapter Six
Zujitsu Fighting Rhythms

One of the truly unique aspects of Zujitsu is its relation to music and rhythms. The first time I saw Chaka perform—using a variety of weapons, wielding them in sync to the rhythms of the music—it connected me in a way no other martial art had done before. Learning how to sync martial arts movements, both empty handed and with weapons, is not present in any other modern martial arts. Although there is now a division in tournaments called Musical Forms, the performances are not quite the same, nor is the training. With my extensive background in music and music theory, this is absolutely the perfect marriage.

Rhythm is inherent in every aspect of life—beginning with the beat of our hearts, to the rhythm of our walk, to the rhythm of a fight. Executing martial arts movements to various rhythms is not a simple skill. It not only requires basic mastery of the movements but also command and understanding of rhythms and their variations. Even some of our advanced black belts with many years of experience, have a very challenging time mastering this aspect of Zujitsu.

Since it is not a common method of training, sometimes the value of this training is not understood by other martial artists. I remember an instance, when several well-known East Coast advanced martial artists were in a group and Sensei Chaka Zulu's name was mentioned. One of them—who shall remain nameless—said, "Oh, the Dancer." Sensei Zulu's response is always, "Yes. Come dance with me!"

I have personally developed and taught workshops presenting these skills at quite a number of martial arts conferences over a thirty-year period. These workshops have become one of my signature statements in the field. I have also performed these skills at many conference demonstrations. Mostly retired at seventy-six and no longer operating our own dojo, my daily morning training routine became a 20-40 minute continuous workout. I would start by wielding my favorite weapons of a short staff (jo), a walking cane or a stone-bead necklace to music emanating from my ear buds. It became one of my most enjoyable daily pleasures.

My husband also does his workout with ear buds and our mutual playlist of over four hundred musical selections. The list includes a variety of musical modes. Some of them are:

Modern Pop: *Levitating* by Dua Lipa or *One More Night* by Maroon Five

Classic Pop: *You Rock My World* by Michael Jackson

Reggae: *Full Control* by Shaggy

Country: *I Can't* by Reba McIntyre or *That Girl by* Jennifer Nettles

Latin and Reggaeton: *Despacito* by Luis Fonsi & Daddy Yankee or *Pa La Calle* by Sofia Kings

Caribbean: *Reach Home Safe* by Damien Marley

Jazz: *Rise* by Herb Alpert

Classical: *Masquerade* by Yuri Ahronovitch & the London Symphony Orchestra

Afrobeats: *Normal* by Burna Boy.

For anyone beginning this training, it is important to choose a slow song with a steady, strong beat.

Chapter Seven
Taking A Leap of Faith

In 1987, I took a leap of faith, quitting my position as a chemistry lab technician at Mt. Sinai to pursue a career in physical fitness. I had already obtained a Masters Degree in physical education but decided I did not want to teach below college level, after student teaching at an elementary school. I had been a lab tech for twelve years and it provided us with a steady income and good medical coverage.

In 1984, I was able to get involved with the Rape Crisis Intervention Program at Mt. Sinai, that was new and innovative for that time. I completed their Advocate Training Program and became an on-call advocate in their ER, once a week. This meant that I could get a call at anytime, day or night to report to the ER, if a rape survivor was being treated. My job was to offer support to her by doing everything from holding her hand, to contacting her family or friends, to giving her information on follow-up support. I believe this program at Mt. Sinai was the first in NYC. However, I did not enjoy the lab work and really wanted to pursue a career I could love.

The fitness industry was in its early stages. Calisthenic classes were being replaced by aerobics classes and strength training was gaining popularity. I secured a position as Aerobics Director at a gym—called the Exercise Training Center—on East 38th Street in Manhattan. Since there were no pre-made aerobics class music tapes at that time, I had to put one together. Everyone was using cassette tapes at that time. I worked on a routine that incorporated my martial arts background with punches, kicks, elbow, knees and stances to music. I practiced until I felt somewhat comfortable.

After my first class, my boss told me the feedback was pretty negative. The participants—primarily women—wanted a dance aerobics class. Unfortunately, my *kickboxing* format was way before it's time. Interestingly enough, a few years later, the Tae Bo craze became popular. So, I began training in dance aerobics with one of the other instructors at the gym. I caught on pretty quickly and my classes became popular. A short while later, the Fitness Director quit and I took over those responsibilities, as well.

It was a great job for two years and we even moved our dojo classes to that facility. However, the large chain gyms—like the NY Health & Racquet Club and NY Sports Club—began taking over the market. Sadly, our gym had to close due to financial reasons. My next position was Wellness Director at the 23rd Street YMCA. Besides teaching classes and coordinating a team of instructors, we held wellness days where I would check members' blood pressure, cholesterol and body fat. I also became a trainer for the national division of the YMCA. I left that position in 1992 and soon after, we opened our commercial dojo on 23rd Street.

I was able to further my fitness education during those years, obtaining quite a few additional certifications. I became a Certified Aerobics Instructor with the American Council on Exercise (ACE) and a Group Exercise Leader with Kenneth Cooper's Institute for Aerobics Research. I attended numerous continuing education programs, including Exercise Programs for Special Populations, Fitness Trends in the '90s, Sports Nutrition, Exercise Programs for Children, Reebok Bodywalk Distance Training and Let's Get Lateral. When Step Aerobics came out, I trained with its founder Gin Miller, obtaining certificates in the basic five-hour Step Reebok Instructional Workshop, Circuit Challenge, Step Interval and Resist-A-Ball.

Although I no longer held a full-time position, I retained my private clients for many years. One of my clients was the artist Lutka Pink. Born in Warsaw, Poland to Jewish parents in 1906, she left for Paris before WWII to pursue her painting career. Sadly, her parents were killed by Hitler. Her work has appeared in countless shows and museums. In her 80s when we met, she now lived at the famed Chelsea Hotel on West 23rd St. I would visit her in her room, go through a fitness routine and then sit while she painted me on canvas. I still have that painting, which I cherish.

To make ends meet, I would travel to several venues every day —from teaching classes at three colleges to private client homes to the dojo. It was a busy time but I loved it all.

Chapter Eight

A Secret Marriage

In October 1989, we decided to make our relationship official and get married. We set a date of April 29, 1990 for a Saturday afternoon affair. Since we were on a very tight budget, we looked for ways to make it a festive occasion without spending too much money. I spent the next six months making all the preparations. Knowing that the actual day would fly by quickly, I made it a point to enjoy every bit of the planning.

Our venue would be the loft home of one of Chaka's black belts, Alan. The space was right on Second Avenue and 7th Street. I hand-wrote all the invitations, indicating the venue was "Chez Alan." My good friend, Joan had a beautiful white dress that didn't fit her anymore, so it became my wedding dress. The food was a group effort, provided by a couple of close friends and my wonderful mother-in-law. She made a huge tray of little salmon cakes that were a real hit. They were gobbled up so fast, that neither Chaka nor I ever got to taste one. I bought decorations and flowers that adorned the whole loft. Since we had several friends who were hairdressers, I was treated to a lovely up-do that made me feel like a princess.

The kitchen in the loft had a peninsula that became the bar and our host, Alan was the bartender. We had one of my oldest friends from college, John—who was licensed to perform marriages—conduct the ceremony. Our friend Marlene, who was a videographer, took video and edited it as our gift. Finally, the most money we spent was on a DJ. His music was great and kept everyone dancing for hours. There were about 75 people who attended. They were of all colors and nationalities. Many were the black belts from our martial arts school, others were long time friends and colleagues.

Usually weddings are a family affair, however I had no one from my family attend. I didn't even tell my parents that we were getting married. This was my secret. I knew they would object and probably not even attend, so I saved myself the grief. Since most of my family perished in Europe during WWII, I only had a few cousins. I decided not to tell them either. I found out a couple of years later that my closest cousin Joan and her husband Neil would have loved to be there but at the time, I assumed otherwise. Fortunately, Chaka's wonderful mother and two cousins did attend. It was great to have them there. Our wedding is a testament that you don't need to spend a whole lot of money to have a super wedding!

Our Wedding Photo

Chapter Nine

Married to My Teacher

Being married to my martial arts teacher has its unique challenges. Whenever I am in class or at a martial arts gathering, I always address him as "Sensei"—the Japanese word for "teacher"—the title that he prefers. He also has a few other titles, like Grand Master and Soke, which is how he is addressed whenever he is in a martial arts setting.

For many years, having him as my teacher was a trigger for me. It brought up memories and emotions from my childhood, when my father was my piano teacher and I was so defiant. In that case, my father relented and had me study piano with one of his colleagues. However, Zujitsu cannot be duplicated and Sensei Zulu cannot be replaced. So, he has been and remains, my martial arts teacher. Over time, I have become more accepting and less triggered by his corrections and even welcome them now.

I have, however, never wanted people to think I got my rank just because I was his wife. To that end, I have always made sure to teach at events—both co-ed and women-only—and to perform in demonstrations. It has been important for me to go out and teach without him, to spread Zujitsu and to establish my own identity.

Chapter Ten
National Women's Martial Arts Federation
Camp Trainer

During the 1980s, I attended almost every summer Special Training conducted by the National Women's Martial Arts Federation (NWMAF). Each year, it was held at a different venue, organized by various members. Participants and instructors were all women, offering various martial arts topics. Many different styles of martial arts were represented. I applied to teach at a few of these camps during the '80s but was never selected.

Finally, in 1993, I was hired to teach. Camp was to be held at Hofstra University in Long Island, NY, coordinated by Linda Ramzy Ranson, a Bronx Fuji Jujitsu practitioner. It turned out to be the largest camp ever with well over six-hundred women in attendance. I was a 4th degree black belt at that time. I taught three different classes: Advanced Self-defense for brown belts and above, Self-defense Without Sight (where techniques must be executed wearing a blindfold) and Defense Against Multiple Attackers. I was both nervous and excited as a first time trainer but the women were so supportive, that I ended up having a wonderful time teaching. It would be only the first of many more occasions as a trainer at these camps. At the Saturday evening group performance, I did a blindfold self-defense demonstration.

I am now a Lifetime member of the NWMAF organization, have taught workshops at a dozen of their summer camps, served as their Board of Director's Chair 2002-2004 and am certified by them as an Empowerment Self-defense Instructor.

Chapter Eleven

Martial Arts Masters of the 20th Century

Chaka and I have attended many wonderful events together, but one of the most exciting was the 1998 gathering of grand masters by Wesley Snipes. It was called Martial Arts Masters of the 20th Century. This was an entire weekend event that began with a Friday evening dinner at the famed Tavern on the Green, located in the middle of Central Park in NYC. A limo picked us up at our 23rd Street dojo for the ride up to the venue. When we arrived, the array and diversity of martial artists in attendance was amazing. Every major martial style seemed to be represented, as well as every nationality.

The masters included Tak Kubota, Douglas Wong and his wife Carrie, Pan Qing Fu, Wen Mei Yu, Kilindi Iyi, Thomas LaPuppet, Steve Muhammad, Bill Ryusaki, Tadashi Yamashita, Fumio Demura, Karriem Abdallah, Hee Il Cho, Ernie Reyes Sr. and Jr., Jhoon Rhee, Henry Cho, Ronald Duncan, Moses Powell, John David, Billy Davis, Leon Jay, Antonio Pereira, Michael DePasquale, Ron Van Clief, Shi Yan Ming, Linda Ranson, Cynthia Rothrock and of course, Chaka Zulu. This amazing mix of martial artists, representing many arts and cultures, was truly historic. It remains to be an iconic gathering, not reproduced. The venue, dinner and conversation that evening are a forever memory.

Saturday and Sunday were spent at City College auditorium, where all the masters received their awards and several outstanding performances were enjoyed. I vividly remember when Jhoon Rhee—who was sixty-five years old at that time—jumped up on stage and pumped out 100 pushups! Although the awardees were mostly male, a few of my tribal sisters also attended in support of their teachers, including Janet Aalfs and Darlene DeFour. This epic occasion was televised on TNT (the network) and can still be viewed on YouTube. Sadly, quite a few of these greats have since passed on.

Martial Arts Masters of the 20th Century
Chaka, Bottom Row, 2nd From Left

Chapter Twelve
Our Journey to China

On Thursday, February 24, 2000, Chaka and I departed New York City for the journey of a lifetime. The trip was advertised in the Pacific Association of Women Martial Artists' newsletter, an organization of which I was a member. It was a delegation to the People's Republic of China of women martial artists. The year 1999 had been a rough year for me, losing both my parents within six months of each other and I was seeking an adventure to rejuvenate my spirit. I took a semester leave from teaching at Queensborough Community College and my calendar was open. What we found proved to be exhilarating and fulfilling, somewhat unexpected, wonderful and validated the Zujitsu Martial Arts system.

Our journey was co-organized by the International Exchange Programs office in Seattle, in conjunction with the China Association for Science and Technology (CAST) in Beijing, China, who were our most gracious hosts. The trip was open to any female martial artists and their spouses. In all, there were eleven women, nine black belts, two white belts and two spouses. The men were my husband and Bill, black belt husband of Nhumey who led the delegation. We also had a travel manager from LIYA and an international guide, Ms. Yan, from CAST who acted as our interpreter. Ms. Yan was a seventeen-year retired officer in the Chinese Navy. She was a strong looking woman and had vast knowledge of all the cultural places we visited. In addition, a local guide joined us in each city. The itinerary covered four cities in fourteen days, including Beijing, Xi'an, Zhengzhou and Shanghai. Our time in each city was divided between cultural activities and visits to martial arts schools.

At each school, we were greeted with much warmth and respect. Hand painted banners, local press media and community locals became commonplace. Smiles from both sides broke down language barriers wherever we went. Our activities at the schools included meetings with instructors and administrators where introductions were made, questions asked and concepts discussed —all through interpreters. Then we would adjourn to the training halls where we performed our arts for each other and sometimes trained together.

Since this was the first delegation of its kind, much of the specific itinerary was modified along the way. Initially, the women were supposed to do most of the demonstrations but after my husband performed his first demo, it became clear that he would do many more. Indeed, he performed at nearly every school we attended, sometimes accompanied by me. What became the greatest surprise for us both was the acceptance and enthusiasm with which we and our art of Zujitsu were received.

One of the best compliments and highlights of our trip was at the Shaanxi Provincial Academy of Martial Arts in Xi'an. First the youth—who were awesome—performed alternately with members of our delegation. Sitting in street clothes on the sidelines and watching, were all the Chinese elder instructors. Then Chaka turned on the music—a jazz tune, called "Down to the Bone." As he started moving to the rhythm, first empty hand and then with a staff, everyone began clapping to the beat and tapping their feet.

As soon as he finished to thunderous applause, two of the elder instructors (in street clothes) stood up and began to *push hands* to the jazz beat. "Push Hands, or Tuishou, is a two-person training routine, practiced in internal Chinese martial arts."—*Wikipedia*. As they moved to the music, it became a dance, each moving, pushing, pulling, trying to unbalance one another. It was truly a moment in history. The audience was exhilarated. Fortunately, I have most of this on videotape, edited into a documentary, currently on my YouTube channel. @zujitsudalaimama

My favorite demonstration was in Zhengzhou at the Henan Provincial Martial Arts Center. Our host was Madam Chen Peiju, a sixty-five-year-old senior coach. She was a slim, strong-looking woman with perfect posture and technique, exhibited as she later performed for us. After changing into our martial arts uniforms, we all entered the large gym. Several Chinese female martial artists greeted us with smiles and we exchanged traditional bows. They were not in traditional uniforms but regular track suits. During our introductions, our interpreter explained that they have over one hundred fifty different kung fu styles in China.

Then we began to alternate demonstrations for each other. Some of the Chinese women were world champions, exhibiting extraordinary skills. I loved how they performed in their track suits. It was not necessary to wear a formal uniform in order to demonstrate or practice their art. When it was my turn to demo, I decided to really challenge myself. Every different style of martial art has its own forms, or katas. These are choreographed movements that are executed in a specific sequence, like a choreographed dance. Instead of performing one of our standard Zujitsu forms, I decided to create one *on the fly*. I began the form and ended the form in the traditional manner but all the techniques in between emanated from my impromptu Zujitsu muscle memory. No one, except Chaka, knew I had just created a new form. The next part of my demonstration was blindfold self-defense. Bill, the other male black belt on our journey, agreed to be the attacker. He towered over me at over six feet so it was a great match. I executed several different defenses against various grabs. Our Chinese hosts clearly loved this demonstration as I scanned their faces during the applause. We ended our visit with Madam Chen teaching us a few moves from her form.

As we traveled throughout this vast country by plane, train, and mini-van, we were continually fascinated by the culture shock we were experiencing. We were at once amazed by the amount of people in the cities. Crowds filled the sidewalks and streets. Everywhere, people rode on bicycles—one of the most common modes of transport. We were delighted when, on one rainy day, thousands of cyclists appeared in brightly colored ponchos, filling the drab streets with blues, reds, yellows and greens. It seemed the skies almost always remained gray, especially in the cities. This is because their most common method of heating was coal. It is this coal that grays the skies and pollutes the air every winter. It was commonplace to see cyclists wearing dust masks.

Another interesting feature was the difference in living quarters. This was most evident as we traveled by train from Xi'an to Zhengzhou. Moving through the countryside, we saw doorways cut into the mountains. They were often in a row and indeed were the entrances into the homes of people who lived in and farmed the area. We were awed by the landscapes of neatly manicured and framed plateaus of rice fields. We often saw these cave dwellers—superior farmers—walking with buckets of water or garden tools.

The cities also exhibited a dichotomy of living quarters. This was most striking in Shanghai, where modern buildings would be right across the street from primitive old huts. Methodically, the old was being replaced by the new. We laughed as wet laundry, from bras to pants, hung all over Shanghai—lamppost to lamppost, window to window, street level and up—right across from newly built high-rises.

Most striking, however, were the plumbing facilities. The common question among us wherever we went was "Are there Western or Chinese toilets?" The Chinese toilet is a hole in the floor with a porcelain base where you place your feet on either side and squat into a horse stance to do your business. No flushing, no toilet paper—no joke! Well, the martial arts horse stance finally came to good practical use. I couldn't resist videotaping Deb Godner—black belt from Coleen Gragen's Kajukenbo school in Oakland—whom we met on this journey and she has since become one of my dearest friends. She aptly demonstrated the horse stance in one of the stalls. Even the *Western* toilets in the trains had footprints on the seats. So, whenever we left our modern hotels, we always carried toilet paper and anti-bacterial hand sanitizer!

We all enjoyed the food, most thoroughly. Nhumey's sister was a chef who had organized a trip the previous year, so we were able to visit many of her recommended wonderful and different restaurants. A few included a Mongolian barbecue, a Muslim place in Xi'an, a Peking duck feast, a Buddhist monk eatery—where everything was made from tofu but looked and tasted like shrimp, scallops, chicken, or beef—a House of Dumplings with every variety imaginable and a Hot Pot eatery—where you choose your food from a huge buffet and cook it in your own pot at the table. This place also served large bottles of wine which held either a scorpion or snake in the bottle. Of course, Chaka tried each one but not me. The Peking duck feast was served, traditionally. First, the perfectly browned and crispy duck is presented for everyone to admire. Then it is taken aside and carefully carved with perfectly thin slices. Finally, it is served with thin crepe-like pancakes and a delicious sweet sauce. What a treat! Also at each meal, beer or *pijiu* (peejo) was served along with bottled water. Indeed, bottled water was the only water to drink or to use to brush your teeth. Tea was always offered as well. At one restaurant, tea was served from a teapot with an arched spout about two feet long, which the waiter expertly poured directly into our cups.

Standing In Front of the Great Wall of China

During our two weeks in China, we visited over a dozen martial arts schools, learned Mulan Fan Boxing in a local Shanghai Park, visited a Cloisonné factory, saw the Peking Opera and the Shanghai Acrobats. We visited Tiananmen Square, The Forbidden City, The Great Wall, the Lama Temple, the Terra Cotta Warriors, the Shaolin Temple, Shanghai Museum and the Jade Buddha Temple.

The Forbidden City consisted of several buildings, separated by large open areas, one after another, going further towards the center building that housed the Imperial Palace and the Emperor's living quarters. Tiananmen Square is a large open space in the center of Beijing. It contains the Monument to the People's Heroes, the Great Hall of the People, the National Museum of China and the Mausoleum of Mao Zedong. Prominent is a huge red wall with a huge photo of Mao Zedong. The square was filled with soldiers who revealed absolutely no facial expressions, totally focused on their severe roles under Communist rules. Tiananmen Square is known for the 1989 student-led protests which were crushed by China's Communist rulers.

The Great Wall is unbelievably long. It is quite challenging to walk up the stairs. Built entirely from stone by hand, the stairs are totally uneven, sometimes close together and sometimes quite far apart. The entire length of the wall is actually over thirteen-thousand miles long and was built over several dynasties. It was originally constructed to protect the country from marauders across the northern border. It is believed that construction began in the 7th century BC. Historians estimate hundreds of thousands of workers died during its construction—due to the harsh conditions—dying from exhaustion, disease, accidents, and severe weather.

The Shanghai Museum is filled with beautiful works of art. As I was wandering through the halls at one point, I realized Chaka was still in a previous room. When I went back, I saw him sitting in front of a stunning painting of a few beautiful tigers. He was born in the Year of the Tiger according to the Chinese Zodiac. The painting was huge, taking up the entire wall. Chaka then asked the curator if it was for sale. Fortunately, the painter had done a smaller version that was for sale! We bought it and it was rolled up and placed in a secure container. When we arrived back home and took it out, we realized it was actually 3 ft. high by 6 ft. long. It cost us more to have it framed than the painting itself. It is beautiful and hangs in our living room over the couch.

The Shaolin Temple is believed to be the birthplace of martial arts. Legend says the Indian monk, Bodhidharma, traveled to China in the 6th century AD, where he found the Shaolin monks, who were weak and unhealthy. He developed Shaolin Kung Fu to make them stronger and fit. When we visited the Shaolin Temple, both Chaka and I found secluded spots where we each executed Zujitsu movements. So, we can now say we trained at the Shaolin Temple! We made many new friends, had a terrific time and validated Zujitsu Martial Arts. The acceptance and excitement we received during the demonstrations of our art of Zujitsu, just reaffirmed our belief, that we are on the right path.

A favorite phrase that both Chaka and I often quote, comes from one of the conference room meetings we had with martial arts masters. "It is not necessary to have more space than a cow takes up in order to train your martial art."

An interesting reflection of our journey was that, although most of the Chinese people had never seen a Black man in person, they displayed no negativity toward him or us as a couple. Indeed, their attitudes were mostly of curiosity, especially regarding Chaka's hair—which at that time, was in medium-length dreadlocks, pulled back into a pony tail.

Shaanxi Provincial Academy of Martial Arts in Xi'an

Chapter Thirteen

Women Warriors Seminar in St. Thomas

After Chaka and I sold the little red house in Woodstock in 2003, we purchased a condo in St. Thomas, USVI. We had been visiting often, staying with his Aunt Olivia and decided we wanted a permanent place. The timing was right, when we found our one-bedroom place at Sapphire Village with a balcony overlooking the marina and a view of the beautiful Caribbean. For many years, Chaka would go down to spend several months avoiding the cold winters in New York. I was still tied down to my teaching schedule at Queensborough Community College, so I would take every opportunity to head down during vacations and intersession. Chaka was teaching at our dojo up on the mountain, where one of his black belts had a wonderful space with our senior black belt instructor, Manuel Benitez.

In 2006, we had about twenty students—all Brown and Black men. Since I always enjoyed training with them whenever I was down at the condo, I decided it would be great for them to meet some of my awesome warrior sisters. We would have a weekend seminar, where all of the instructors would be women and all the students would be men. I knew I would need to bring some superior women martial arts instructors for this seminar.

So, to join me in the instructor lineup, I invited:

Janice Okamoto from California, a senior black belt student of Small Circle Jujitsu founder, Wally Jay. She was the director of Camp Danzan Ryu and at five-foot-three, she could easily slam down a large man.

Gaby Roloff from Germany, a senior student of Remy Presas founder of Modern Arnis, who was magic with her two sticks.

Sandie Benevides, a Tae Kwon Do instructor who could do a jumping side kick to take your head off from two feet away.

Anne Nepsky McCabe from Flagstaff, Kenpo Karate stylist—with the crispest punches and kicks— who had a talent for musical forms.

Priscilla Horton, our Zujitsu black belt—also a student of Qi Gong—who led us in a closing self-massage session.

Each one of these women had been training in their martial art for at least twenty-five years. It was an impressive group! A few other folks also came down for the event, including Dennis Dias and George Arrington, both excellent martial arts instructors, as well. Everyone rented condos at the complex for a few days to participate in our beach workout/picnic and to explore beautiful St. Thomas. The seminar went off without a hitch. Each woman kept everyone captivated, as she taught her segment. All the men were respectful and eager to learn from these amazing female warriors. The entire trip was a great success.

Priscilla, Janice, Anne, Zosia, Sandie, Gaby

Chapter Fourteen
Meeting A Great Icon

Chaka and I have done quite a bit of traveling, sometimes martial arts related, sometimes not. On this trip to California, he met one of the few martial artists he always spoke of and idolized. On May 18, 2006, Chaka, I, and our black belt Eric Howard, boarded a 7 a.m. flight (at JFK airport) to Oakland, California. We had been invited to teach at Camp Danzan Ryu. It was a smooth flight on Jet Blue, with personal TV sets at every seat. Due to the time difference, we arrived at 10 a.m. and were greeted by our host, Janice Okamoto, and our friend Leslie. After collecting our baggage, we drove to a Japanese restaurant for lunch. There, we were met by Dennis Dias and his son Matthew. It was great to see him again after the St. Thomas trip. The lunch lasted a couple of hours, as we chatted and dined on sushi and sake.

The next morning, we all took off for Camp Danzan Ryu. This martial arts camp was founded in 1984 to honor the memory of Professor Henry S. Okazaki (born in 1890) who developed a system of self-defense Jujitsu and Restoration, called Kodenkan Danzan Ryu. In 1929, he established the Nikko Sanatorium of Restorative Massage, where he earned fame as a physical therapist. His system is based on the belief that if you know how to injure, you also need to know how to heal. Camp Danzan Ryu strives to keep alive his spirit of Ohana—the Hawaiian word for family—and Kokua, meaning to share.

My friend Janice had been co-director of the camp for many years and invited Chaka and I to come teach. En route to camp, she planned a short detour to a tourist destination, called The Mystery Spot. As the brochure says, "The Mystery Spot is an area about 150 feet in diameter located in the redwood forest just outside of Santa Cruz, CA. Within the Mystery Spot you will be baffled as the laws of physics and gravity cease to exist. Discovered in 1939 and opened to the public in 1940, it has amazed and perplexed hundreds of thousands of visitors from all over the world. Many return again to experience the puzzling variations in gravity, perspective, height and more." It truly is a unique experience. As we walked through the cabin there, I felt myself losing all sense of balance and gravity. I had never experienced anything like it before. It was quite an unnerving and unique feeling.

After driving up some winding roads, we finally got to camp, a beautiful site in the Santa Cruz Mountains—about 60 miles south of San Francisco. Camp Danzan Ryu is on several acres of wooded land. All the structures are wood and rustic. There is one main building that houses the kitchen/dining room and another building with an area that is matted for the classes that have throws and morning yoga. Two cabins with several small rooms and communal bathrooms house the instructors. Several more cabins up the hill provide bunkbeds and bathrooms for the camp participants. There is also a swimming pool, a large field with bleachers and a campfire area with a small stage.

The next couple of days were full of activities and friends, both old and new. During our visit, there were twenty-three instructors leading both adult and children workouts, representing a variety of martial arts styles. This camp is a great opportunity to try out various martial arts styles. If you are a beginner, you have a chance to decide what style fits you best to begin. If you are advanced, you have a chance to incorporate additional/new techniques into your own repertoire.

A few offerings and their instructors, were:

Judo and Krav Maga, Denise Gonzales
Aikido, Pat Hendricks
Danzan Ryu Jujitsu, Tony Janovich
Kajukenbo Kung Fu, Robert Maschmeire
Eskrima/Kali/Arnis, Nito Noval
Shorin Ryu Karate, Jim Silvan
Kung Fu, Janet Gee
Kenpo Karate, Anne McCabe-Nepsky
Seifukujutsu Restoration Therapy, George Arrington
Adrenal Stress Scenario Training, Meredith Gold and Mike Belzer.

Eric and I participated in several of these classes offered and especially enjoyed a walking cane class with John Lofton. Chaka sat and watched the entire class and this became the beginning of the development of the Zu-Cane, that is now part of our system. The Zujitsu Walking Cane system is different than others we have seen posted online or in person. Additionally, Chaka has personally carved and wood burned various scenes on many canes, that are used by students and friends. His artwork has been well admired.

Our Zujitsu classes were scheduled right after breakfast on Saturday morning. Chaka was first. The room was packed with close to fifty students who were all curious to learn more about Zujitsu. As usual, Sensei Zulu did not disappoint. He shared some of his unique training exercises including the Bumble Bee, Nudging and One-Arm Blocking. I taught the next class and continued with the Sticky Paper Chase drill. This drill uses an 8.5 x 11 piece of paper that is cut in half, so it is larger than palm size. I love using colored paper but white printing paper is fine. For this drill, with the paper on your palm and your palm absolutely straight—no cupping allowed—the object is to begin moving while not allowing the paper to fall. You must keep your arm and your feet moving. It can be quite challenging. This drill increases sensitivity and has you learn how to remain in contact, while redirecting someone's energy. In a fight, defending in this manner requires less effort and energy.

On Saturday evening, we had a traditional campfire complete with sing-a-longs, stories and S'mores. This is a yearly tradition and is especially fun for the youngsters. After lunch on Sunday, we returned to the San Francisco area to unload the gear and rest. On Monday, we visited with our old friend, Anton Muhammad at his dojo in Oakland where a kid's class was in progress. It's always wonderful to watch youngsters learning martial arts. The lessons they learn are invaluable and not just the physical lessons. They also learn self discipline, focus, good sportsmanship and teamwork. Later, we did some sightseeing at Fisherman's Wharf and had their famous, delicious, traditional clam chowder, served in a sourdough bread bowl. Whenever we are in the area, that is one of our favorite meals.

Finally, it was time to head over to Alameda for Sensei Zulu's seminar where he would finally meet Professor Wally Jay, a martial arts icon. The seminar was to be held at the dojo of Lee Eichelberger, one of Wally Jay's senior instructors. Chaka's main teacher, Frank Ruiz had passed away about ten years prior to this trip. For someone who had been training since he was ten and was now sixty-seven, it wasn't easy to find another teacher.

His main teachers now, were the Chinese Kung Fu movies he would watch. In the 1970s and 1980s, Chaka would go down to Chinatown several times a week to watch these films. He would choose different techniques and bring them back to incorporate into his repertoire.

Wally Jay, founder of Small Circle Jujitsu, was eighty-nine years old and had many more years of training under his belt. For years, Chaka had expressed his wish to meet and train with him. Upon arriving, we were greeted by Jay and his lovely wife, Bernice, who was also a martial artist. Unfortunately, his health and energy level did not permit him to get on the mat but he expressed to Chaka that he wished he could join in. He did, however, give Eric and me a firsthand demonstration of a *pinky lock redirection* with his palm. He was well known for manipulating his students' fingers to cause pain and placing them in submissive positions. I felt honored to be taken down to the floor by his famous techniques. It was a very memorable evening and altogether a great trip to California.

Chaka, Wally Jay, Zosia, Eric (standing)

Chapter Fifteen

Women Warriors Teaching Tour in Israel

In December of 2009, several of my warrior sisters and I went on an adventure to Israel. We were invited by Yudit Sidikman to participate in the El HaLev Circle of Strength Bat Mitzvah Celebration. Located in Jerusalem, El HaLev is dedicated to women's self-defense and empowerment.

The instructors in the group besides myself, included Janice Okamoto and Gaby Roloff. Others included Laura Armstrong from Canada (a World Stick Fighting champion), Jamie Zimron from California (a world-traveling, peacemaker, Aikido master) and Sherry McGregor from Florida, a World Karate champion and my demo partner. Also in attendance, were Susan Williams (RIP)—a Women's Army Corps Veteran—and Elizabeth Wexford, both from Massachusetts, both USA Goju Karate. Our journey through Israel was packed with adventures. Our days were filled with both cultural tourist attractions and volunteer workshops, where we shared our martial arts and self-defense skills with various groups.

The day after our arrival, we were separated into partners and sent to different venues to teach self-defense. My partner was Yael. She was a Jujitsu black belt, an Israeli woman who was a volunteer at El HaLev. Our task was to go to Givon prison in Ramla, about forty-four kilometers from Jerusalem. This prison is a detention center, primarily for undocumented migrants. We were to teach self-defense to a group of women. These women were all from different countries, had escaped persecution and entered into Israel, illegally. We were told that no physical self-defense skills were allowed to be taught since they were in prison. We had to rely on various empowerment skills to help make these women safer.

I was already quite disoriented, having just arrived in this foreign country. Yael drove us there in her car and almost got us into an accident, which did nothing for my stress level. When we finally arrived, the prison looked ominous. The bare walls were topped off with a surround of barbed wire. We were escorted through security, where they checked our credentials and searched our bags. Then we were led into an open area with a few tables and benches.

The incarcerated women were led in by two officers. They were different ages, races and from different neighboring countries. None of them were violent criminals and their only crime was entering Israel without a permit, so they could escape persecution in their home country. Most of them could not speak Hebrew or English. It became clear this would be a big challenge for us.

The general public thinks that self-defense only refers to physical force to prevent oneself from being harmed. However, Empowerment Self-defense addresses many more aspects. In most cases, true self-defense begins way before any physical contact. It begins with awareness of one's surroundings, avoiding conflict, listening to your intuition, carrying oneself with strong posture, eye contact, using one's voice tone and volume, speaking with assertive language, setting boundaries and yelling forcefully. We spent the next ninety minutes imparting this information to these women through our body language, smiles, bits and pieces of words, role-playing and woman-to-woman understanding. It was an amazing experience I will never forget.

That was only the first of several more opportunities to share our knowledge and definitely one of the most rewarding. I left there wondering what the future of these women would be, hoping that our workshop would help them survive. My trip had begun with one of the most intense experiences. I was anxious to hear how the other groups had fared. Apparently, none of them had experienced anything quite so intense. I was now ready for whatever came my way!

We loved exploring the Holy City of Jerusalem. On the first night of Hanukkah, we walked through the winding streets of the Old City to the Wailing Wall—also known as the Western Wall. The ultimate place for prayer, it is the holiest site in Judaism today. Groups are separated, men from women, left and right, waiting to go up to touch the wall and pray. It is customary to insert a piece of paper with a prayer request between the stones of the wall. Twice a year, the Rabbi retrieves them and buries them in a Jewish cemetery.

I savored leading a yoga practice at the Mitzpe Shalem outlook over the Sea of Galilee. The scenery was breathtaking and expansive. It was silent, except for the wind. I looked out at the dozen beautiful women in front of me and took a deep breath. Then, I began to slowly lead them through some basic yoga poses. Slowly loosening up each joint, moving with our breaths. Balancing with the stillness of the moment, as we moved into Tree Pose and Dancer Pose. That image will forever remain in my mind.

There was some adventurous driving up to the site of a fierce battle, during the Yom Kippur War at Mt. Bental. Of course, never missing an opportunity to train, we had a knife defense workout at the top. It was fun hiking through the Tel Dan Nature Reserve that was lush and green. We wandered through the Old Jaffa flea market, purchasing whatever trinkets and mementos we could buy.

We all enjoyed floating in the Dead Sea. The water there is so full of salty minerals, that it literally causes you to float without even trying. It kind of feels like you are laying in a lounge chair, sipping a cocktail. Then it was time to make the climb up and up the Snake Path to Masada. The Masada is an ancient fortification that overlooks the Dead Sea. It is actually on top of a large rock plateau. Founded in the first century BC, it holds legends of mass suicide during the first Jewish-Roman War. It is a UNESCO World Heritage Site and a popular tourist attraction.

The plan was to wake up at 5am to begin the long winding path up to the top to witness the spectacular sunrise. The walk up would take over an hour. It was an arduous walk with uneven terrain but we finally made it! We were all so ready to see the sunrise. So *where is the sun*, we all asked. *Nope.* No sunrise. The weather gods were just not being cooperative. It remained cloudy and overcast that entire morning but it was a great climb!

It was so fun taking a camel ride but very dusty in the desert. Those big animals easily held two of us at a time. Then, we were ushered into a Bedouin tent for lunch. Carpets covered the ground, as we all sat down. Several different foods were served on large trays. It was delicious, as all food is in Israel.

Most emotional for me, was visiting the Yad Vashem Holocaust Memorial. As I walked into the entrance, seeing the photos of crowds enjoying life before the war hit me hard. The genetic trauma of my ancestors killed by Hitler, filled me with tears and sorrow. But I was glad for the museum and the remembrance. I was also able to donate a few photos of my relatives (who were killed) for their archives. "Never Forget" is the motto. I am outraged by the present day Holocaust deniers who say it never happened.

We shared our skills with populations—which included at-risk boy and girl teens, children, people with special needs, incarcerated illegal immigrant women at the Givon prison, Orthodox girls, and Ethiopian refugees. Although we had our El Halev sisters interpreting from Hebrew to English for us, our language challenges continually followed us, as we encountered many who spoke neither language. However, we were all able to communicate in the universal languages of body movement, eye contact, voice tone and volume, high fives, and hugs.

Perhaps most impressive was our visit to the Budo for Peace dojo in the small, unrecognized Bedouin village of Abu Querad in the Negev desert. Budo for Peace is a non-profit organization that brings together young people from conflict areas to learn and practice a traditional Japanese martial art. They do this in order to learn its values and apply the skills toward breaking down fear and building trust between peoples. The village had a population of about three-thousand, electricity provided by unreliable generators and no constant water supply. The dojo was nothing more than a concrete building with some donated puzzle mats on the floor. It had been in operation since 2006, with a dedicated group of students—boys and girls—ranging in ages from six to eighteen years of age. They practiced the art of Shotokan Karate under their teacher, Hazem Abu Quidar, who had been training for sixteen years. They had just promoted their first black belt student.

What we witnessed there was most extraordinary. Even with all the most obvious challenges, these boys and girls exhibited skills of an incredibly high level. Their self-discipline was evident as they stood quietly at attention when we arrived and slowly entered their humble dojo. Their eyes were bright with excitement and smiles adorned their faces, as Budo for Peace's Chairman,

Danny Hakim, made his introductions and explained the program to their visitors.

Then it was time for the youngsters to demonstrate their art for us, and *WOW*—they sure did! Their techniques were short and clean, stances strong, chambers tight and punches crisp. Completely focused, they moved through their forms with grace and determination. One young girl demonstrated her self-defense skills against two bullies in a scenario on her way home from school. These youngsters easily won our hearts.

Then, it was our turn to demonstrate our skills for them. They were a great audience, attentive and clapping loudly for each of us. I demonstrated a few self-defense techniques, wearing a blindfold —one of my favorite demos. Everyone in the dojo could feel the connection and the magic that was happening. It was a truly inspiring event, that reaffirmed: it's not about how many medals we win or how many students we have or how large our income. It is about the gift we have to share with the world, about the lives we can touch through our art, to make it a better place to live for us all.

Zosia Demonstrating Blind-folded Self-Defense at Budo For Peace Dojo

The Group at the Budo For Peace Dojo in Israel

Chapter Sixteen
Zujitsu in Atlanta

In 2010, while Chaka was at our condo in St. Thomas, our Zujitsu black belt Eric Howard invited me down to Atlanta to teach at a seminar featuring several other male instructors. Two of Eric's sons—Zujitsu black belts, Kyle and Saquan—and our black belt, Richard Irving would also be going down. I consider these men to be our family and we had been training together since the 1990s. They are all Black men who are intelligent, well educated and well respected in their communities.

I also invited one of my sister-warriors—black belt, Kerry Kilburn from Virginia—to come down a couple of days early so we could explore Atlanta. One of our first visits was to the incredible Atlanta Aquarium. In 2010, it was the largest aquarium in the world and now, is still the largest aquarium in the United States. It features hundreds of species and thousands of animals across its several major galleries. It is also home to the only whale sharks in captivity (the largest fish in the ocean). Since Kerry was a professor of biology, I ended up having a personal professional guide to explain all the various forms of aquatic life we were seeing.

Our next visit was to the Dr. Martin Luther King Jr. National Historical Park site. Established in 1968 by his wife, Coretta Scott King, it is the official memorial dedicated to his legacy. The entire site covers thirty-five acres, including the visitor center, an old firehouse that now contains a gift shop, the "I Have a Dream" International World Peace Rose Garden, the International Civil Rights walk of Fame and more. We went to the visitor center that features the multimedia exhibit *Courage to Lead,* which follows the parallel paths of Dr. King and the civil rights movement. It is a beautiful exhibit that elicited many emotions from us both.

Our final stop was to Mary Mac's Tea Room. According to their website, "Back in 1945, Mary MacKenzie opened Mary Mac's Tea Room near Peachtree Street on Ponce de Leon Avenue. In those tough days right after the end of World War II, enterprising women in search of a living, some of them mothers widowed by the war, were establishing restaurants all over Atlanta. At the time, a woman couldn't just open up a restaurant, so many female proprietors used the more refined Southern name of "Tea Room." Mary Mac's Tea Room was one of 16 tearooms in Atlanta and seated 75 guests. Today, Mary Mac's is the only original tearoom that remains."

Walking into this restaurant was like walking into the past. There are several rooms with the architecture and furnishings reminiscent of the Old South. Just reading the menu made my mouth water. Some of my favorites included Fried Chicken, Chicken and Dumplings, Shrimp and Grits, Fried Green Tomatoes, Lightly Fried Okra, Golden Fried Hushpuppies, Black-Eyed Peas, Collard Greens, Mac and Cheese, Tomato Pie, Georgia Peach Cobbler, Sweet Tea and Cream Soda. The food was delicious and worth the trip!

The seminar was scheduled for the following day, to be held in a large gym. It was filled almost exclusively with Black men, martial artists of all ranks. The event had been organized by Tanwir Sahib, with Papasan Canty, two well-known martial arts masters. When it was time for my segment, I knew I did not want to focus on strength or size. Most men are stronger and larger than most women and it is not always the best strategy to fight on those terms. As women, a smaller man, or an elder, it behooves us to fight on our own terms. The strategy of being soft, connecting, feeling and redirecting the force of strength that is coming at you is a wise, yet challenging strategy, especially for men. So I retrieved my envelope of colored paper for the Sticky Paper Chase drill. First, I explained the drill to the gym full of men. Then, I spent a few minutes demonstrating the drill. I started off with my dominant left hand and then switched to my right hand and back again. I know I made it look easy. I had been practicing. Then, I directed everyone to begin. It was fantastic. Paper was dropping to the floor all over the gym. There was a lot of laughter and frustration. It was a very real challenge for these men. Everyone enjoyed it and had a unique learning experience. I have taught this drill at many events, always with a positive response.

Later in the day, after the seminar, a performance for family and friends was held at a nearby auditorium. I did an impromptu demonstration using my walking cane as a defensive weapon to The Black Eyed Peas song "Union." Kyle, Saquan and Richard assisted me, attacking both empty-handed and with knives, as I defended, utilizing the help of my cane. Fortunately, Kerry was in the audience and able to videotape the entire demo which appears on my YouTube channel @zujitsudalaimama. It was a wonderful day and a great way to end a memorable weekend.

Chapter Seventeen

Hall of Fame

One of my proudest achievements in the world of women's martial arts, is the AWMAI Hall of Fame. This organization—the Association of Women Martial Arts Instructors—was inspired and founded in 2000 by my dear friend, Dara Masi, Hakko Densho Ryu Jujitsu master. Its mission is to "provide high-quality education, training, and support, as well as opportunities for networking, advancement, and professional recognition, to women instructors and business owners in the fields of martial arts and self-defense." I proudly served as their Executive Director from 2008-2014.

In 2012, Certification Director Janice Okamoto and I founded the AWMAI Hall of Fame. We were both tired of seeing all the male operated organizations constantly awarding their (martial arts) buddies just for showing up at their events. So, we decided we would make our Hall of Fame award criteria really representative of an important achievement. In order to apply to receive this award, an instructor must have thirty-plus active years as a martial artist. This is not easy to achieve and requires "a great deal of commitment, dedication, and passion," especially in a male dominated profession.

At that time, I personally knew one-hundred, three female instructors who fit this criteria. I invited all of them. Thirty-one of them accepted, attended the conference and were inducted into the first AWMAI Hall of Fame. We had an amazing group! There were women who had only been training and teaching in their own towns, well-known women, such as Kathy Long, Arlene Limas, Graciela Casillas, and Cookie Melendez, sixty-plus-years awardee

Bernice Jay, and dear women—who have since passed—Barbara Feldman, Marjory Allingham, and Peg Strain. As of 2025, over seventy-five women with more than thirty to sixty years experience, have been awarded for their service. See their website at awmai.org.

Zosia and Janice Okamoto

Chapter Eighteen
Our Chosen Family

Martial arts brought Chaka and I together and has played a huge role in keeping us together. Many people who do not practice martial arts may believe it is a violent activity. Indeed, every country that has ever had to defend itself against foreign invasion has developed a martial art for protection. Often, these arts would have to be practiced in secrecy. Some were disguised, like the Brazilian art of Capoeira. This art appeared to be a dance, with various percussion instruments and distinctive rhythms. The Pacific Islanders disguised their art in the Hula dances. However, martial arts is mostly practiced so that the fight can be avoided. The practitioner is ready to defend, if necessary.

Traditional martial arts in the U.S. were mainly brought here after WWII by servicemen stationed in Okinawa. Besides learning how to fight to defend oneself, emphasis is on development of self discipline, physical health and spiritual growth. Violence plays no part in traditional martial arts training. Actual training requires a lot of control, both physical and emotional, to avoid injuring your partner and yourself. In order to advance, you must attend class a minimum of three times per week for at least one hour, often two hours. Lifelong martial artists realize that their training covers many aspects and is a 24-hour endeavor.

As one progresses, it is important to have complete trust in your training partner. Often, you are as close to your partner as you would be with your spouse. An amazing camaraderie develops with your dojo (martial arts school) partners, whom you now refer to as your dojo brothers and sisters. It is a unique relationship that must be experienced to be truly understood.

A phenomenon of many—if not most—martial arts schools is that they are mostly segregated by White, Black, Asian and Latino. The Asian schools are also separated into Japanese, Okinawan, Chinese, Korean, Filipino and Vietnamese. However, when I joined Chaka's dojo, I saw a very multiracial school. This aspect was very appealing to me and it has remained this way ever since. Perhaps the segregation is somewhat fueled by the fact that people look for a school close to their homes and unfortunately, we still live in a country where few truly multiracial neighborhoods exist. Perhaps it is because people feel an affinity for their own cultures and are seeking to find strength within their *own people*. Whatever the reason, it has never been that way with our martial arts system.

Since the majority of our students have been twenty-plus years younger than my husband, they have often looked to him as a surrogate father. Indeed, several have either lost their fathers or were abandoned by them, so Chaka easily fits the role. He calls them all his sons and daughters. Some students—who are offspring of older students—have even become grandchildren, like Saquan and Brandon. For me, as an only child, having dojo brothers and sisters has fulfilled me beyond my dreams. These are men and women who have been training with us for over thirty years.

Chaka's longest student is Manuel (Manny) Benitez in St. Thomas, who has been training with him for over fifty years. Manny, his wife Pauline, sister-in-law Jenny and her son Kevin are our family there. My other dojo brothers and sisters are wonderful humans, like Alan, Richard, Kenton, Douglas, Nick, Sky, Alex, Ray, Stephane, Barry, Priscilla, Anne, Liston, Rod, Nyah and Osandu. And of course, Eric, who affectionately calls me "Mommy Dearest" (no relation to the melodrama with Joan Crawford!). Then there are my own personal students, who followed me after attending my self-defense class at Queensborough Community College. Five young men continued training at our Forest Hills home dojo. Five young men, representing five different nationalities: Marco, Omar, Willis, Yi, and Ben—Puerto Rican, Black, Dominican, Chinese, and Jewish Orthodox, respectively. This is our multiracial chosen family of dedicated, trustworthy, outstanding individuals whom I call Family.

Black Belt Class in Forest Hills Dojo, 2013

Chapter Nineteen

A Great Loss

Chaka has promoted many students to the rank of black belt. He has also acquired some, who were looking for a new teacher or different style. One afternoon in 1998, I received a phone call at our dojo on 23rd Street. The caller said he was an instructor from San Antonio, Texas who was from the Moses Powell lineage. Chaka had trained with Powell in jujitsu and he was well-known. The caller, Lee Goodridge said he was in NYC with three of his black belts and "would it be possible" to pay a class fee and come train that evening. Of course, we welcomed them and the class that night was fantastic.

Lee, already a great martial artist and a 6th degree black belt, immediately decided Chaka would be his new teacher. That was the beginning of a wonderful relationship. Just about every year Chaka and I would go down to San Antonio to teach a seminar and visit with Lee and his students. At that time, he was living with Jo, a Mexican physician, who had a large home that reminded me of a hacienda. She and I became fast friends and we always looked forward to our visits. Unfortunately, since Lee was a Black man, whenever Jo's family would visit, he had to pretend to live in the extra apartment at the hacienda. Chaka and I hated this situation but it certainly was not our decision to make. Sadly, their relationship did not last and a few years later he married a French woman.

Lee and I became the best training buddies. We always looked forward to any occasion to train together because we both learned so much from each other. Not only did we visit him in San Antonio but he and a few of his black belts would join us at other events.

They came to upstate New York for Camp Suigetsu followed by training at our Woodstock home. They also joined us in Orlando, Florida at the World Head of Family Sokeship Council conference in 2001. Several Zujitsu Black Belts, including Lee, received awards at their banquet. He came down to St. Thomas a few times, including our 2008 Zujitsu Training Week, where we had quite a crowd.

Lee was five years older than me, a soft-spoken, mild-mannered, church-going man and a wonderful martial artist. We became like brother and sister. In 2013, when I was planning my retirement from university teaching, Chaka and I decided to leave NYC and move to San Antonio. The plan was to buy a home large enough to house our dojo and that Lee and Chaka would grow old together. We went down and found a place that seemed perfect. Of course, it was large, like everything in Texas. Even though I needed to finish out the term in December, we closed on the house in July. We would use the *formal* living room as our indoor dojo and fence in the yard to build an outdoor dojo.

Before we left San Antonio, Lee had been experiencing some health issues after returning from a trip to Africa. The last time I saw him was in his hospital bed but he was expected to make a full recovery. Since Chaka and I had already planned a trip down to our condo in St. Thomas, we went down for a few weeks. Around midnight July twenty-fifth, the phone rang at our condo. It was Craig, one of Lee's black belts. Lee had suddenly passed away. We were both shocked and tears began flowing.

How could this happen? What about our plans to be together? He was supposed to have a full recovery. Over the next few months, we began preparations for our move. We already had our home and his students knew us, so hopefully we could still move forward, as planned but without Lee. We ended up living there for just over three years. We had our dojo at the house but it wasn't the same without Lee. Our large home also required constant upkeep and too many repairs. We decided Texas just wasn't a good fit for us. So, we continued moving westward and in 2017, we moved to Southern California.

Lee and Chaka

Chapter Twenty
Is Blood Thicker Than Water?

Both of us have lost many blood relatives. Chaka's entire family on his father's side is unknown to him, except that they came from North Carolina. Most likely his ancestors were slaves. He lost his only sister and only son to gun violence.

Thankfully, his first cousin, Denese, has been a consistent support to this day. Although she suffered with her own demons as a youngster, she emerged a strong and compassionate woman. I appreciate her no-nonsense approach to life. We will be forever grateful to her for the love and care she showed Chaka's mother. She has always been as close to me as any blood relative and I love her, dearly.

Chaka's mother, Mama Drina, was one of the kindest women I have ever met. From the moment we met, she showed me nothing but love. Her childhood was spent in St. Thomas, USVI. She was one of eleven children, born to a Puerto Rican father and St. Crucian mother. Although she was a lovely, attractive woman, when Chaka's father left, she never remarried. When I met her, she lived in one of the *project* buildings in the Bronx. These consisted of several high-rise buildings constructed as low-income public housing. The buildings were fourteen stories high with about ten apartments on each floor. We would visit her often, always bringing some groceries or other gifts.

I vividly remember her building. The lobby was bare where we were buzzed in. Most often, we would take the elevator up to her second-floor apartment. The hallway was stark with plain, secure doors to each apartment. Often as we were leaving, we would walk down the stairs. I remember the strong stench of urine in the stairway. It was so different from where my parents lived, moving to a townhouse in Forest Hills, Queens in 1966. It was just a grim reminder of the different opportunities afforded our opposing cultures.

Mama Drina's two-bedroom apartment was always immaculate. She would anticipate our arrival, cooking some of our favorite meals—fried fish and fungi. Fungi is a Caribbean dish of corn meal, also known as polenta, with bits of okra mixed in. She loved when I would bring her green beans I had grown in my parents' backyard. Her walnut cake was absolutely delicious. She was a marvelous seamstress and knitter. Her couch was filled with dolls, adorned in the beautiful dresses she had knitted for them. As she aged and arthritis set in, her fingers were unable to continue knitting. Sometimes, we would visit her at the Senior Center, located on the ground floor of the adjacent building. She loved having us there and would introduce us to all her friends, so proud of us. She lived to be ninety-five years old.

I lost most of my family when Hitler invaded Poland. Others have passed away or were estranged. My father's older sister, Beba, was quite a bit older. She lived in a large apartment on Bennett Avenue in Washington Heights, Manhattan. She was a strong, opinionated woman who was very independent. She was also a wonderful seamstress and made a beautiful green dress for me when I was about twelve. Her husband, Emil, was a lovely man. She had one daughter, Joan, who was quite a few years older than me.

Many say Joan and I shared a strong physical resemblance—same blue eyes and blonde hair. According to her daughter, Ellyn, we both share direct, honest, no-nonsense personalities. Unfortunately, since I was many years younger, we only developed a close relationship when I became an adult. It was then, that she took on the role of my older sister. Sadly, she was an avid chain-smoker and passed from lung cancer, three days after her 76th birthday in 2010.

Joan married a wonderful man, Neil. He was tall and mild-mannered. He loved to smoke his pipe and had great-smelling tobaccos. Neil was a head of the news department at CBS for over forty years until he retired. Joan and Neil had two daughters—first Ellyn and two years later, Marci. Ellyn is a teacher of little children, four years old at a Yeshiva. Her specialty is arts and crafts. Marci has worked her way up at CBS to a producer of a food segment in the weekend morning show. Their apartment, a small, three-bedroom, one-bath in Riverdale, is still home to Ellyn and Marci.

I fondly remember going to their home, every Passover. This Jewish holiday is a celebration of the story of Exodus—how our Jewish ancestors were led out of slavery from Egypt by Moses. Although our family was not religious at all, we would celebrate the traditional Seder every year. The dining room table was squeezed into a small area where ten of us would be seated.

The table was set beautifully with all the traditional foods mentioned during the Seder ritual. These included:

The Matzo (unleavened bread), the Z'Roah (a roasted shank bone) and an egg—symbolic of the blood of a sacrificed lamb, marking their houses, so that the *destroyer* would *pass-over* and spare their first born.

Maror, horseradish or bitter herbs symbolic of the Jews suffering in Egypt.

Charoses, a delicious mixture of chopped apple, nuts, cinnamon and wine, symbolic of the mortar used by the Israelites in Egypt.

Karpas, a bit of vegetable to be dipped in salt water.

In addition to the food, sufficient wine—always Manischewitz—was provided to fill four cups for each person. The Seder ceremony, executed to its full extent, can take a couple of hours to complete. However, our *unreligious* but *traditional* family always performed the very shortened version, anxious to get to the feast Joan would prepare. Some favorites, were her fantastic brisket of beef and kugel—a delicious noodle dish. Dessert was her famous chocolate cake roll (filled with cream) and a plum cake.

My fondest memory of one such occasion was in 1979. At the table, were my parents, Joan and Neil, Aunt Beba, Marci, Ellyn, cousin Jeffrey on Neil's side, his boyfriend Charles and myself. I had brought one marijuana joint with me. All of us cousins told the elders we wanted to take a walk after dinner. So, we went down to the street and all shared this one joint. It was great and we all laughed about how we fooled our elders as we all got high on this one joint! Sadly, Jeffrey died of AIDS not long after but Ellyn, Marci and I still reminisce about that Passover.

Ellyn has become one of the closest people in my life and we have a phone date, early every Saturday. She and Marci have always been supportive and they love Chaka, as well. Indeed, after my parents passed away in 1999, Chaka was always welcomed into their home. We spent many evenings with Joan and Neil. They even came to the grand opening of our first commercial dojo in Manhattan in 1993. Their relationship with us was always confidential from my parents. Ellyn recently told me she and her sister could never understand why Chaka was not invited to their home, when my parents were there. Joan tried to explain it to them and said that it was a secret they needed to keep.

Cousins Neil and Joan With Us

Chapter Twenty-One
Our Legacy

Without any children of our own, due to various circumstances —what is our legacy? As fate would have it, in 2016, Chaka's estranged daughter, Keenya, found me on Facebook. It had been since the early 1980s that she had disappeared from Chaka's life. She had fallen into the despair of addiction and we lost all contact. Fortunately, since then, she had recovered and was now happily married and living in New York. The reunion with Chaka was heartwarming, although long distance, as we had already moved away from NY. They managed to speak often until her past caught up with her and due to her failing health, she passed away in June, 2017. However, we also discovered she had given birth to two sons in 1990 and 1991. As she was unable to care for them, due to her addiction, they were brought up by other family members. This news was very exciting for Chaka. He had grandsons!

Soon after, grandson Tino contacted us. We found out that he had a very rough childhood, shuffled around, unsure of whom exactly were his blood relatives. However, in spite of his upbringing, he seemed to emerge without any negative resentments. We began regular communications with him, letting him know we never even knew he existed but now thrilled to be connected. He was living in South Carolina, working as the manager of a local nightclub.

We were all anxious to meet, so we invited him to our home in California. Arrangements were made for him to spend two weeks with us. I know we were somewhat concerned about the visit. Two weeks can be a long time, having someone stay in one's home. *Would we get along? How would he feel about his past? Would any resentments about the past surface?* Fortunately our fears were erased, the moment he stepped into our home.

We had seen photos of him but were not quite ready for the six-foot-two, two-hundred, forty pound, muscular man who turned out to be as gentle as a big teddy bear. The visit turned out to be a love-fest for all three of us. Many hours were spent talking, well into the late hours. Every morning was an opportunity for Chaka to begin Tino's martial arts training. We took him to our favorite restaurants, to the beach, and to my Chinese brush painting class. Chaka and I were amazed at his open heart, especially after hearing about his tumultuous upbringing.

The two weeks flew by too fast. We all wanted more time together. I absolutely melted when it was time for him to leave and he hugged me in his loving, strong arms and called me "GrandMa." I never thought that would ever happen for me. To this day, I am so grateful for him and I don't think I could love him any more, if he were my *blood* grandson. He has visited us several times since then and we speak often. He is now married to Jessica, a wonderful young woman and has his own financial/life insurance business, called Gordon Legacy. He will be our legacy.

The following is the tribute he composed for Chaka's eighty-fifth birthday, December 28, 2023:

Can you imagine meeting a living legend in your own family? Well, that's exactly what happened to me back in 2019, and let me tell you, it was one of the most mind-blowing experiences of my life! Before that day, I was oblivious to the legacy that awaited me. It wasn't until after my mother's death that I got to take a deeper look into the past of my family tree. Little did I know that my grandpa was an absolute force to be reckoned with. He had been quietly leading an extraordinary life, completely unknown to me. But oh boy, once I met him, everything changed! My grandpa is not just any ordinary person; he's a Grand Master, a Mentor, and a Marine. His life stories are like chapters from an epic novel that keep you on the edge of your seat. I didn't know that this mysterious man was the source of my love for martial arts and creative thinking. Each step along the journey to meet him filled with uncertainty and wonder, it felt like sailing uncharted territory in the open sea. Anticipation was building inside my body like a tsunami until fate finally brought me face-to-face with him.

Two souls united by blood yet separated by time. As our eyes locked for the first time, an electric current surged through my veins. It was as if destiny had conspired for this very connection to occur. In his presence I felt both humbled and empowered simultaneously. It was an encounter I will never forget filled with emotion, discovery, and an overwhelming sense of belonging. In that instant, I realized that this newfound relationship would shape my life forever. Now the fun begins. He began to train me. Almost a century of martial arts and combat knowledge crammed into intense all day sessions. My grandpa's expertise left me spellbound. Every move he made seemed effortless yet packed with power and precision.

Now with every passing day, I dive deeper into what it means to have a legacy, and how it shapes the lives of others. My grandpa's legacy continues to inspire me daily, reminding me of the strength and resilience that lies with our family. This journey has brought immeasurable joy and love into my life. So cheers to uncovering hidden treasures within our own families. Those living legends who shape our very existence. May we all have the chance to embrace them with open hearts and learn from their wisdom. And guess what? Today is my grandpa's birthday. Join me in celebrating this incredible man who has enriched my world beyond measure. Let's shower him with love, respect, and wishes for many more years of health and happiness. Happy Birthday Grandpa Chaka Zulu.

Grandson Tino with Grandpa Chaka Zulu

Chapter Twenty-Two
Legacy Recipes

Mama Judith's Blintzes

For the Crepe Batter: 4 eggs, 6 tablespoons of flour, 2 1/4 glasses of milk, then 1/2 glass more
For the Filling: 1 egg, 1 lb. Farmer's cheese, sugar to taste
Make crepes in good, non-stick crepe pan.
Fill with cheese filling. Add blueberries (Optional).
Roll and pan fry in butter.

Mama Judith's Knedle

Polish Knedle, traditionally, are dumplings with a plum filling. This recipe is just the dumpling without the filling.
Mix one package of Farmer's cheese, 1 stick of butter, 1 cup All Purpose flour and 1 egg. Form into small dumplings and boil in water for 10 minutes.

Mama Judith's Meringue Cookies

 4 egg whites at room temperature, 1/2 cup sugar, 1/2 tsp. cream of tartar, 1-2 tsp. vanilla or almond extract and 3/4 cup chopped walnuts
Beat egg whites and cream of tartar with electric mixer in a deep bowl 'till fluffy
Add vanilla & sugar—beat to combine, then fold in nuts
Preheat oven to 300°
Grease dull side of aluminum cookie sheet
Spoon glops onto cookie sheet
Bake 30 minutes. Turn down to 250° for another 45 minutes
Watch color. If browning, turn down oven.

Mama Drina's Walnut Cake

2 1/2 sticks softened unsalted butter, 3 cups white sugar, 3 cups AP flour, 16 oz. sour cream, 16 oz. chopped walnuts, 2 tsp. baking powder, 2 tsp. baking soda, 2 tsp. cinnamon, 3 tsp. vanilla, 4 eggs

Mix sugar & eggs well, add rest of ingredients and mix well. Put in baking pan. Bake for 60 minutes in preheated 350° oven.

Mama Drina's Fried Fish Gravy

Sauté sliced onions until caramelized, add Ketchup & Red Wine Vinegar, salt. Mix to taste.

Cousin Joan's Plum Cake

1 stick unsalted butter softened, 1 cup sugar, 1 cup flour, 1 tsp. baking powder, 2 eggs, 8 small or 5 large plums, cut into pieces. Beat softened butter & sugar until smooth. Add flour, baking powder, eggs and blend together. Put batter in buttered round baking pan or 9" square pan. Push in plum pieces. Top with cinnamon sugar. Bake one hour at preheated 350° oven.

Cousin Joan's Chocolate Roll Cake

For the cake: 6 eggs, separated, 3/4 cup sugar, 1/3 cup unsweetened cocoa, 1 1/2 tsp vanilla extract, dash of salt

For the filling: 1 1/2 cups heavy cream, 1/2 cup confectioners sugar, 1/4 cup unsweetened cocoa, 1 tsp. vanilla

Grease bottom of a 15 1/2 x 10 1/2 x 1" jelly roll pan. Line with parchment or waxed paper. Butter paper. Preheat oven to 375°

Beat egg whites at high speed to form soft peaks. Add 1/4 cup sugar, 2 Tbsp. at a time. Beat to form stiff peaks.
Beat yolks at high speed adding remaining 1/2 cup sugar, 2 Tbsp. at a time. Beat 4 minutes.

At low speed, add cocoa, vanilla & salt, just until smooth. Gently fold chocolate mix into eggs whites just until blended. Spread evenly in pan.

Bake 15 minutes, just until surface springs back.

Sift confectioners sugar on a towel. Turn cake out onto the sugar. Peel off paper. Roll up cake, jelly roll fashion. Cool completely on a rack, seam side down, for at least 1/2 hour.

Filling: Combine ingredients in a medium bowl. Best with electric mixer until thick. Refrigerate.

Unroll cake, spread with filling within an inch from the edge. Re-roll. Place seam side down. Wrap in foil and freeze.

To serve: Optional, sprinkle with confectioner's sugar. It can be served frozen or remove from freezer 1/2 hour before serving. It thaws as soon as it is sliced.

Chapter Twenty-Three
Our Dojos

During the entire time since I met Chaka, until we moved to California in 2017, we have had a brick and mortar Zujitsu dojo. Actually, we have had many. We had to move quite a few times because, in New York, rent is expensive. Unless one is willing to operate a large commercial school and take in many students, rent becomes prohibitive. That was never Chaka's nor my inclination. From the time we met at his 2nd Avenue dojo in 1981 until 1993 we had eight different dojos spaces.

In 1993, we rented a loft over a comic book store on East 23rd St. Gregg, our black belt instructor who had moved to California, flew in and sanded the beautiful wooden floors. One entire long wall was painted white brick and two large windows faced the street at one end. We had a grand opening, attended by many friends, students and even my cousins Joan and Neil. We spent a couple of good years in that space and built up our school.

After our lease was over, we moved across the street to a larger dojo. This place had a big dressing room with a shower for the men and another for the women. The greeting entry was spacious with a couch and an office space in the corner. The windows were large and faced the street. One of our brown belts, a wonderful artist, painted our logo and martial arts figures on the windows. We had another grand opening and many more festive occasions. We also had many awesome classes. We trained there for five years but when it was time to renew our lease, the landlord asked for double the rent. It just wasn't possible for us to pay that high rent.

Shortly thereafter, we decided to close our commercial dojo and to only hold classes for brown and black belts at our home dojo in Forest Hills, where we had moved after my parents passed away. I also conducted a weekly class for my students—from Queensborough Community College—who had continued their training. Although the ceiling was quite low, it was an intimate space that had everyone working on close-quarters training. Since only brown and black belts could attend, the level of practice and learning was quite advanced. When the weather was warm enough, the class was held outside, out the back door, in the rear driveway/ garden area. The fenced garden grew my tomatoes, green beans, zucchini, cucumbers and more. This driveway is also where I enjoyed teaching my QCC students the Jo. The Jo, a fifty-inch wooden staff, is my weapon of choice and I still practice with it, six days a week.

Simultaneously, we have had five more outdoor dojo spaces for our school since the first one, the original Dojo in the Woods. We trained by the stream at the Woodstock home, every morning at our spot by the ocean in St. Thomas, on the communal backyard driveway in Forest Hills and on the training devices Chaka and black-belt Ken built in the yard in San Antonio. Training in many different spaces has always encouraged new and creative ways to move. It also reinforces the ability to adapt. Occasionally we lost a student due to a move but if so, they were just not for us. Martial Arts training is not always *comfortable*, sometimes inconvenient and requires a level of dedication to excel.

**23rd Street Dojo Sign Painted For Us By
Our Brown Belt, Pamela**

**Chaka and Manny Benitez Training on the Beach
in St. Thomas, USVI**

Chapter Twenty-Four
Good Karma

In September of 2018, two of our black belt instructors from New York, Eric and Nyah, came to California to visit us in our new home. As two of our senior students, we all had a wonderful time training together, again. After a few hours of training, it was time for lunch. Nyah really wanted some Thai food. *No problem*, we have a great little family run place, Khao Hom Bistro. When we walked into the small restaurant, only two other single men were at tables. One was in a corner, the other in the middle. He was a White man, wearing a muscle shirt that showed off his chiseled physique and several tattoos. As we walked towards the empty corner table, I greeted him and he responded in kind. Then he and Chaka greeted each other, as well, and he continued to eat his meal. The four of us, then proceeded to order a table full of food and fresh coconuts. I mean, there was no empty spot on that table. Fish, chicken, seafood, vegetables, fried rice, *oh my*. We all began to eat and the food was delicious.

So, the man next to us finishes his meal and gets up to pay his bill, then comes over to Chaka, and says, "Thank You for your service." As a former US Marine, Chaka always wears a cap with the USMC emblem and he has a USMC tattoo on his forearm. As the guy turns to walk out we noticed the back of his shirt says, "Stand for Something." Right after he leaves, the waitress comes to our table. She says, "You know, he just paid for your bill." We all stopped eating and looked at each other in shock. "What did you say?" I asked. She repeated and added, "I thought he told you." *OMG!* We couldn't move or speak. Then Eric jumped up and ran out. A few minutes later, he returned with our benefactor. As we each got up to thank him, I felt my eyes well up, as I gave him my heartfelt hug. He stayed long enough to tell us about his time in the service, overseas where he was shot, had a tracheotomy and almost died. Before he left, he once again thanked Chaka for helping to pave the way for younger servicemen. His name was Nick. That's what is called *Paying it Forward*. May his beautiful good Karma follow him on his life path.

Chaka, Eric, Zosia, Nyah After Training at Dojo Under the Sky

Chapter Twenty-Five
Finding Sifu

Chaka and I have always loved dogs. However, because we traveled so often, we never got one of our own. About a year after COVID began, we decided traveling was no longer a wish for us. We had sold our condo in St. Thomas and thought this might be a good time to get a dog. Many of our neighbors (in California) have dogs and there's a great walking path right outside our door. Neither of us knew much about the different breeds but we wanted a small-medium-sized dog, that was a rescue.

For weeks and weeks I went online and applied to organizations that had rescue dogs available. Finally, we were accepted to adopt Jenny. She was an adorable-looking, black and white dog with features similar to a beagle. Her foster mom arranged to bring her over one July afternoon in 2021. We waited all afternoon and she finally showed up at 6pm. Jenny looked just like her photo. Unfortunately, her foster mom didn't have much information to give us about her background. Jenny seemed happy in our home. She was running around, getting acquainted with her new surroundings. Her foster mom left at 7:30pm. I had prepared for our new dog, buying food, bowls, toys and a dog bed.

Jenny slept the whole night and I took her for a walk in the morning, happy she was potty trained. When I returned, I was sitting in the kitchen with her, when Chaka walked out of the bedroom towards the kitchen. All of a sudden, Jenny began to growl and bare her teeth. She had been fine with him since she arrived but now was clearly not. Her aggressive behavior triggered Chaka's PTSD. This was not a good situation. We tried to relax her but she just wasn't going to budge.

Hoping it was just temporary, I took her out again, this time for a ride in the car. I needed stop by a friend's house to pick up a CD he had for me. We pulled up in front of his house. As he began walking towards the car, Jenny again began baring her teeth and growling. I now had a suspicion that Jenny's past did not include a positive relationship with men. When I finally called her foster, my suspicion was confirmed. I was terribly upset that we had not been told that Jenny had only been fostered by a group of women and had no contact with men. Indeed, it was possible she had been abused by men in her past. I was heartbroken but knew we could not keep her. We called her foster and gave her back that evening. I was in tears and swore I no longer wanted a dog.

The more I told my friends about our situation, the more I heard from them that the best solution would be to get a puppy. A puppy would learn to love us both and come with a blank slate. In less than two days, Jenny had left her hair all over our home. It made me think that for my next search, I would be looking for a hypo-allergenic dog, that did not shed. I narrowed my search and began looking online. Apparently, there are many scammers out there, looking to take your money but never delivering the dog. Prices for these pure breeds also sounded outrageous, with promises of sending the dog from another state. I finally settled on the AKC (American Kennel Club) website that seemed legitimate. However, I was not going to send for an out-of-state dog. I was looking for a dog within driving distance of our California home.

One day, as I was scanning their website, I saw an ad for Mini Schnauzer puppies in Oceanside, California. This was only about fifty miles from us. I called the number and discovered that Lakeesha was an ER nurse and her husband, John was a Lieutenant Colonel in the U.S. Marines, stationed at Camp

Pendleton. This Black family lived near the base with their two teenage daughters and their two Mini Schnauzers, Luke and Lola. Apparently, the two dogs had done the deed and now they had a bunch of puppies that were five weeks old. The situation seemed meant-to-be and fit our needs, exactly. A few days later, we drove down to see the puppies. There had only been one female, already sold and five males still available.

When we met the family, we immediately felt comfortable, as former-Marine Chaka bonded with Marine John. The puppies were adorable and their *doggy* parents, friendly. Both of us gravitated to the puppy with the red collar. He was just a little fluff ball, mostly black with white eyebrows and white feet. He would be ours and we named him Sifu Silverfoot. Sifu is a Chinese Cantonese word (meaning *master* or *teacher*), used in the martial arts. It is similar to the Japanese word *Sensei*. Three weeks later, we picked him up. He was so small that Chaka held him in one hand. It was a love fest from the very beginning. He snuggled in Chaka's lap for the ride home.

For the first six months, he lived in a play pen in our living room during the day and in his crate in the bedroom at night. Both of us spent hours training him. We socialized him with other dogs once he turned four months old and had all his shots. We never left him alone for an entire year. It wasn't difficult since COVID was still very much alive and kicking and no one was socializing. He turned four years old in the summer of 2025.

Although Schnauzers do not shed at all, they have hair that grows fast and needs grooming. I took him to a groomer, twice when he was little. Then my friend, Glenn told me he grooms his own dog and I should try it. So, I bought the necessary tools, grooming table and watched a few videos on YouTube. I started slowly but quickly got the hang of it. Now, I bathe him in the shower with me and cut his hair, regularly. It's a great bonding experience and a money saver, too. Sifu loves other dogs and people. His favorite activity is going to the dog park, so we can play fetch. He just wants to run and retrieve the ball, over and over. Chaka loves giving him massages and Sifu loves it, too. Chaka says it calms him down. He is our therapy dog. Sifu has brought much love and laughter into our home and is definitely an important part of our family, now.

Sifu

Chapter Twenty-Six
The Art of Martial Arts

Chaka's View

Ever since studying the history of the martial arts, every master that I ever read about was also some sort of fine artist. They were either a calligrapher, wood carver, sculptor or painter of some sort. I guess that might be a natural extension of the martial arts. I started by building environments for my dog and my birds. Then one day, a student of mine was in the street and some junkie was trying to sell stuff. He had this set of carving tools to sell. My student thought I might like them and bought a whole bunch of them for $5.00. I had no idea what to do with them but it gave me some incentive to try to carve.

I was living in the 2nd Avenue dojo at the time and I built myself a little desk in the corner of the dojo where I could set up my tools. Then, I started carving anything I could get my hands on. I would find wood on the street and just carve it into something. I'd either hang it up in the dojo or give it to one of my students. I created quite a few pieces—all sizes and shapes.

One of my students, who had a hair salon on St. Marks Place, wanted to display them in his shop. I loaned him several pieces, including a large eagle. Unfortunately, a buffing machine he was using on the salon floor overheated and caught fire when he stepped out. All my artwork in his shop was destroyed. However, I still had quite a few pieces that I displayed and sold at several art fairs.

In my eighties, as wood carving has become more difficult for my hands, I use a wood burning tool on my latest pieces. For the last several years (2020s), I have been wood burning on walking canes, that I have sold to students and neighbors.

My View

Art, as defined in the Oxford dictionary, refers to "the various branches of creative activity, such as painting, music, literature, and dance." The martial arts are not just about fighting someone but the execution of movement, timing, flexibility, speed, gracefulness. This is most evident in the forms or katas, that vary with each martial art style. Karate forms tend to have only about twenty movements, while kung fu forms can have over 100. Zujitsu has taken this one step further, by combining musical rhythms with martial arts movement in a unique form of training.

Before the common use of photography, paintings and drawings were the way to illustrate techniques and pass them down to the next generation. Although the Shaolin monks are known for their martial arts, they also practiced painting, calligraphy and other arts. When we visited the Shaolin Temple, an entire section was dedicated to life size paintings and sculptures of monks in various martial positions. We also saw these wall paintings at other martial arts training schools.

My husband's artistic talents have always amazed me. In the mid-2020s, Chaka gave me a beautiful hand-stamped leather computer case—picturing a tiger and a dragon—for my 76th birthday. He seems to always be engaged in creating something. His amazing focus is also evident when he engages in martial arts training. My other creative modes of expression are playing the piano, Chinese brush painting and gardening.

I purchased a wonderful keyboard that feels and sounds just like a grand piano. I'm focusing on playing Chopin Waltzes and basic Jazz tunes. When I was a child, resenting having to practice every day, my parents used to tell me that *one day* I would *appreciate* knowing how to play. Of course, they were right. Even without playing for several years, the muscle memory in my fingers and my trained ear, has made playing again very enjoyable and less of a challenge than I expected.

My tribe of martial arts warrior sisters also has many women who excel in other modes of artistic expression, besides martial arts. A few notables are:

Beth Holt, Shuri Ryu Karate and Arnis, Pottery Artist.
Kim Ivy, Tai Chi and Qi Gong, Watercolor and Acrylic Painter.
Kore Grate, Kung Fu and Judo, Tattoo Artist.
Michelle Manu, Lua Martial Art, Hula Dancer.
Michele Benzamin-Miki, Aikido and Iado, Fine Artist: Paint and Pencil.
Janet Aalfs, Shuri Ryu Karate and Arnis, Poet Laureate.
Lara Chamberlain, Tiida Ryu Karate, Asian Brush Painter.
Wasentha Young, Tai Chi and Qi Gong, Mosaic Artist.
Michelle Pleasant, Kajukenbo Kung Fu, Painter.

Several have also excelled at the written word, publishing their books. Notables are:

Dr. Michelle Manu, *The Archetype of the Woman Protector, et al.*
Helen Yee, *I Belong Here*
Marilyn Fierro, *The Limitless Spirit of the Martial Arts, et al.*
Graciela Casillas, *The Lioness Within*
Andrea Harkins, *The Martial Arts Woman, et al.*
Lauren Taylor and Nadia Telsey, *Get Empowered*
Cathy Chapaty, *No Pouting in the Dojo* and *Searching for Grasshopper.*

We are a creative tribe!

Chapter Twenty-Seven
Zujitsu Dojo Under the Sky 2025

Our last indoor dojo was at our place in San Antonio in 2017. We now train in our dojo under the sky right outside our doorstep. It's a beautiful spot, along a walking trail, overlooking an expansive meadow. I love how I can freely swing my weapons. I rarely wear my martial arts uniform, choosing instead to train in the workout clothes I wear, walking my dog Sifu before I train. We are fortunate to have spectacular weather, most every day. If it rains, we train inside or take a day off. Several of our black belts have visited us here. They are our family and always welcome. Their visits are always energizing for everyone. We always look forward to those occasions. Tino still trains with Chaka whenever he visits.

As native New Yorkers, we have always been accustomed to living in a diverse community. Moving to this community in Southern California required us to adjust to a different environment. Laguna Woods is a 55+ gated community with a total population of 17,342.

According to Data USA, Census Atlas Orange County, the largest ethnic group here is White at 68.1%, then Asian, 23.7%. Hispanic, Non-Hispanic, and Other Hispanic follows. The Black/African American percentage is 0.7% or approximately 121 people. Notably, the racial breakdown of the U.S. is 58% White, 20% Hispanic, 13% Black, 6% Asian or Pacific Islander and 3% Other. The significance of this breakdown is not only reflective of the socio-economic disparity between ethnic groups but it has also had an interesting cultural effect.

As a former U.S. Marine, Chaka has always adhered to the adage: *Once A Marine, Always A Marine.* This is especially evident in his self-discipline towards his martial arts training. Every day, except Sundays, Chaka is out the door at exactly 8:00 a.m. to begin his daily martial arts training in our Dojo Under the Sky. I usually join him after Sifu's walk. Since our home is situated next to the walking trail, many residents walk by every day, while we are training. We always make it a point to say "Good Morning" to everyone who walks by.

When we first moved here, many people were hesitant to respond. However, after seeing how consistent we have been, all the *regular walkers* greet us, both. What is most interesting is that most of the White residents often ask us what we are doing. "What is that exercise you are doing?" Or "Is that Tai Chi? I've never seen it done that fast." My response usually is "It's a martial art called Zu-Chi." The Asians, however, mostly respond with thumbs up or "beautiful", or "good work." They all know exactly what we are doing. I would also note that the majority of folks walking on the trail in the mornings are Asian. This reminds us of our trip to China where every morning, people would either be training their martial art or ballroom dancing, in the parks or in the street. We rarely see any of the one-hundred, twenty-one Black folks living in our community.

Chapter Twenty-Eight

In Black & White

The world is not black and white. Life is not black and white. Humans are not black and white.

The world is full of colors. Humans are all shades of flesh, from very light to very dark. Why do some people believe that color defines a person or that lighter is better than darker?

Chaka has told me that when he was a boy, he really wanted to be a scientist. His mother told me he was a total bookworm, always reading, always with his head in a book. Unfortunately, as a Black boy in Harlem in the 1940s, education was not a priority. Rather, it was denied. How many other Black boys and girls have been denied an education? Who knows if one of those children could have discovered the cure for cancer?

Fate and martial arts brought us together. We are love in Black and White. Love knows no boundaries. Love happens when you least expect it. Feelings cannot be denied. Of course, we have our disagreements, like any other couple. Chaka sometimes says that I drive him crazy. My response is "It's a short drive!" But we are still together after over forty-four years. We cannot go back. We will not go back. Our country must not go back. It's time for Dr. King's dream to become reality. May we all "be judged by the content of our character, not the color of our skin." And I add, "nor for our religious beliefs."

In Black & White

About Zosia Gorbaty

Zosia Gorbaty is a 9th degree Black Belt in the martial art of Zujitsu. She has been training since 1976. She has conducted martial arts seminars at over 50 events and schools in twenty states. Zosia has been a frequent trainer at the Pacific Association of Women Martial Artists camps, National Women's Martial Arts Federation (NWMAF) camps, Camp Danzan Ryu, and the Association of Women Martial Arts Instructors (AWMAI) conferences.

She served as Board Chair for the NWMAF 2002-4, and as Executive Director for the AWMAI 2008-14. Zosia has a Masters Degree in physical education from New York University, and worked as a fitness professional for many years. She was an adjunct professor at Adelphi University, and Bronx Community College, and Queensborough Community College teaching accredited courses in self-defense, traditional karate, and yoga from 1983-2013.

Most recent interviews include Emmett's YouTube Channel and Andrea Harkins' Martial Arts Woman podcast. She is a recipient of the Silver Life Achievement Award from the World Head of Family Sokeship Council and is featured in their book. Most notable awards include the Masters Hall of Fame, AWMAI Hall of Fame 40+ years, and Van Clief and Dacascos's 2022 Ultimate Warriors Hall of Fame. In 2024 her articles and photos were featured in the 14th edition of the *Deadly Arts of Survival* magazine and the Spring edition of *Martial Arts Masters* magazine.

About Chaka Zulu

Chaka Zulu is a 10th degree Black Belt and founder of the modern, eclectic art of Zujitsu. He is a Veteran of the United States Marine Corps where he served from 1956-62. He has been teaching martial arts for more than sixty years, with thousands of students around the world.

He has been referenced in several publications, including *The Handbook of the Martial Arts* by William Logan, *Martial Arts Traditions, History, and People* by Corcoran and Farkas, *Black Heroes of the Martial Arts* by Ron Van Clief, *Official Karate Magazine, Black Belt Magazine,* and *Karate International*. He appeared in the legendary documentary *The Warrior Within*, seen opening the film relating a story of when shortly after his discharge from the U.S. Martine Corps some guy attempted to rob him. As he says, "The guy went to the hospital, and I went home."

Zulu was one of the honored masters at The First Tribute to the Martial Arts Masters of the 20th Century, produced by Wesley Snipes. In 1992, Grand Patriarch Peter Urban awarded him a 10th degree black belt. He has been officially acknowledged by the World Head of Family Sokeship Council as the Soke, head of the Zujitsu Ryu system, and has been inducted into several Halls of Fame.

Resources

1. NYC Dept. of Records and Information Services

2. Wikipedia

3. archives.sva.edu

4. www.quora.com

5. integralyoga.org

6. LAtimes.com

7. Getting Lost in the Hippie Caves of Matala Crete: Nothing Familiar; Bridgette and Jake

8. Warrior Women, 3000 years of Courage and Heroism, Robin Cross and Rosalind Miles

9. YouTube channel @zujitsudalaimama

10. marymacs.com

11. awmai.org

12. Oxford dictionary